A Century of Petroleum Transport

Graham Edge

Roundoak Publishing

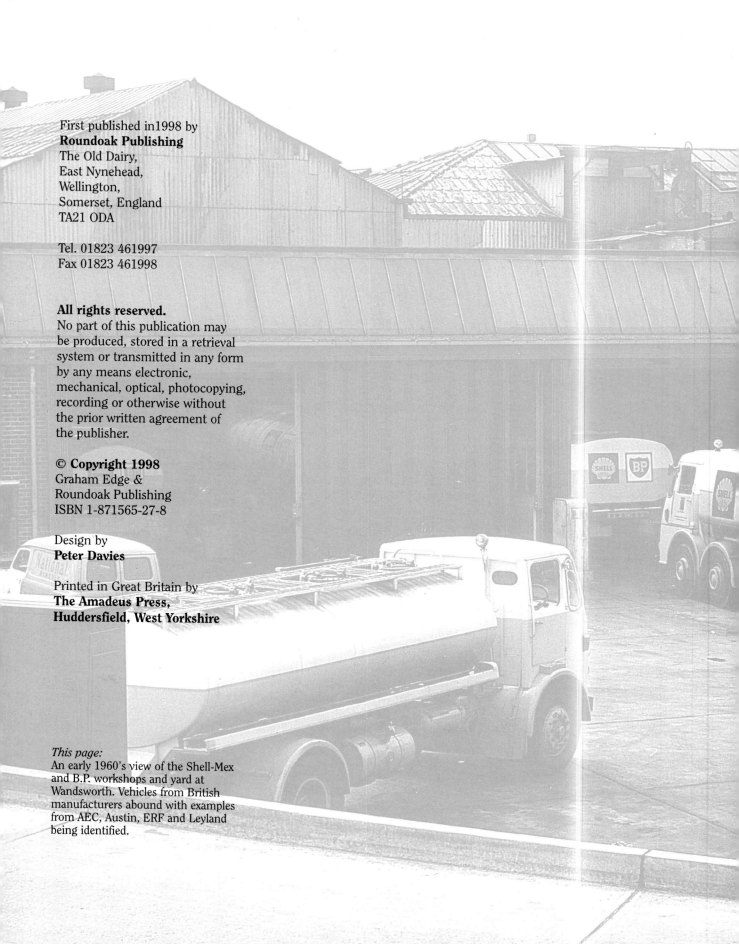

First published in 1998 by
Roundoak Publishing
The Old Dairy,
East Nynehead,
Wellington,
Somerset, England
TA21 ODA

Tel. 01823 461997
Fax 01823 461998

Design by
Peter Davies

Printed in Great Britain by
**The Amadeus Press,
Huddersfield, West Yorkshire**

This page:
An early 1960's view of the Shell-Mex
and B.P. workshops and yard at
Wandsworth. Vehicles from British
manufacturers abound with examples
from AEC, Austin, ERF and Leyland
being identified.

Contents

Acknowledgements

The British oil and petroleum industry has a long history of partnerships and joint ventures. This book about the transportation of its products by road is an appropriate testament to that fact. It is a compilation of photographs sourced mainly from the archives of the companies featured, and this is probably the first book in which Great Britain's leading oil and petroleum producers have been featured together.

The idea for this volume was prompted by a visit to Texaco's head office to view their photographic library for material for a separate project. Enquiries were made of the other oil companies for access to their archives and an excellent response was obtained from them. The results are here for all to see. My thanks are due to all the people who arranged for these photographs to be made available to me, and who also provided details about their respective companies. They also approved the chapter introductions and suggested suitable amendments where appropriate.

All the following individuals have been most helpful and my grateful thanks and appreciation is due to them:

Robert Wine, Brendan Lomax and Margaret Humphrey of BP, along with Jane Dobson and her colleagues at the BP Archive at the University of Warwick.

Dave Burns, Alan Harper and Kim Creed of Conoco/Jet. Keith Aubrey and Michele Covington-Jones of Esso. Pauline Barclay of Fina. Christine Beale of Gulf. Roger Newstead of Mobil. John Brown and Paul West of Shell. David Robinson and Alison Low Madigan of Texaco. Clarissa Killwick, Amanda Long and Paul Rand of Total, along with Mike Doherty and his colleagues at Total's Nottingham Terminal. They and the driver, Gerry Hallam, were most helpful and co-operative when I visited them to learn about their operations and procedures.

Special thanks must also go to Vic Allen, formerly of Texaco, who loaned me several photographs from his own collection. He also provided a wealth of information about tanker design, capacities, operations and vehicles. What a marvellous memory he has.

Arthur Ingram kindly loaned photographs which have helped in filling-in gaps in the pictorial story, and also assisted me in the identification of one or two makes of lorry which were before my time.

Peter Davies has once again unselfishly contributed material from his own impressive collection and has been working very much behind the scenes getting this book to press. Thanks also go to to Jilly Davies for her contribution at the keyboard.

Colin Newbould, formerly of Chevron and VIP, kindly loaned me material from his own collection which was vital for the Gulf chapter.

Gordon Baron and Roslyn Thistlewood searched through the library at the British Commercial Vehicle Museum Trust at Chorley - since relocated back to Leyland - for several gems of photographs.

If anyone who helped in any way has been omitted, then please accept my apologies.

Graham Edge
Swaffham Prior
June 1998

A Dedication

**To the memory
of my sister**

**Josephine
Marie
Coles**

The transport of oil and petroleum by road has become a massive operation as the twentieth century has progressed.

No doubt many people associate the growth of the fuel market with the large increase in car ownership in Great Britain in the past 75 years and the corresponding demand for petrol. However, the oil industry, as such, actually pre-dates the invention of the internal combustion engine. Long before petrol was recognised as an important fuel, oil was in use as an industrial product.

Oil was used as a lubricant with superior properties to those based on animal and vegetable fats. Lamp oil, similar to paraffin, was an important commodity used in many homes and offices as a means of providing lighting before firstly gas, and later electricity, gave the means of illumination.

In those days petrol and other light distillates were often burned off as waste by-products of the crude oil refining process. Nowadays oil is an important prime source of energy and the many products obtained from it provide the means of propulsion for road, rail, air and marine transport in addition to its lubricating properties. It is also an important raw material for plastics and chemicals manufacturing and the bitumen remaining after refining is used as a road surfacing material.

The oil industry in Great Britain started over 100 years ago and because at that time oil reserves had yet to be discovered in or around the British Isles, the product was imported. This situation persisted until the mid-1970s when crude oil from underneath the North Sea was brought ashore.

Because, from the outset, the oil industry was international it led to the formation of multi-national companies which have expanded and grown into massive organisations with cash turnovers running into billions of dollars. However, the retailing of petrol, diesel, fuel oil and lubricants is only the final sequence in a chain of activities which require very large capital investments. Whilst satisfactory returns and profits can be made, the risks are also great and crippling losses may be suffered if incorrect decisions are made.

The oil and petroleum industry has a rich heritage in Great Britain. Some of the major well known companies are American owned and they initially set up subsidiaries here to market and sell lubricants or lamp oil. Others were established here and have become major players in what is more than ever a multi-national industry.

Through the years they have sold several brands of petrol, many of which are now only fond memories. All these companies have used a variety of liveries and images to promote and advertise their products and some of these were the results of partnerships and joint marketing arrangements.

In addition to operating their own fleets of road tankers they all rely upon authorised distributors to sell their products. Most of the distributors have traded with their respective supplier for many decades and are important links in the supply chain to isolated farms and communities, in addition to domestic consumers.

Petrol stations, with which all motorists are familiar, have changed out of all recognition over the years. Even forty years ago most service stations sold several brands of petrol. They were operated by the proprietor, usually with the help of his family, and would also

offer lubricants and maybe car servicing and repair facilities.

Now the service stations are much larger and whilst some are still run as a family business, many others are owned by the oil companies themselves and all retail just one brand of petrol and diesel.

They usually feature a convenience shop as well selling a variety of goods

ranging from a bunch of flowers to a fresh sandwich. But even this is changing. Since 1985 the major supermarket chains have taken an increasingly large share of the market where lower prices rather than brand loyalty attract the purchaser.

This book is a record of the British oil and petroleum industry's road transport operations from its earliest times to the present day. For readers of a certain age it recalls those tankers from commercial vehicle builders no longer in existence, liveried for some brands of oil and petrol which are also just memories. For younger readers it gives some insight of how things used to be. To everyone it will hopefully bring pleasure and enjoyment, showing how the road tanker has evolved and providing a window into the operations of these well known companies. Not least of these being the safety considerations involved in the transporting of hazardous liquids.

Above: Oil deliveries, 19th Century style.
Below: A modern petrol tanker.

The British Petroleum Company PLC

The origins of BP date back to 1901 when William Knox D'Arcy, a wealthy businessman, obtained a concession from the Shah of Persia to explore for and exploit his country's oil reserves. Excluded from the agreement were the northern Persian provinces adjacent to the Russian border.

Persia was a huge territory with no developed infrastructure of roads and communications, the terrain was difficult and weather severe. Problems were encountered with the many hostile native tribes which added to the

difficulties in exploring for oil and no commercial quantities were discovered for several years. By 1905 D'Arcy's original financial resources were exhausted and he sought additional funding. This was forthcoming from the Burmah Oil Company and in May 1908 the syndicate was rewarded with commercial discoveries of crude oil in south west Persia. This was the first large oil find in the Middle East, leading to the emergence of the region as a major oil producer.

In the year of 1909 the Anglo-Persian

Oil Company was formed to develop the oilfield. The Burmah Oil Company held 97% of the ordinary shares with the remainder owned by Lord Strathcona, who was the company's chairman.

From the outset the aim was to build a vertically integrated oil company which was involved in all aspects of the business. A refinery was planned at Abadan, near the Persian Gulf, and construction was completed in 1911. The crude oil was transferred by pipeline from the oilfield which was some 140 miles distant. Anglo-Persian encountered several technical problems in producing marketable products from Persian crude oil. These stretched its finances and because there were no immediate prospects of establishing its own international marketing organisation a ten years contract was agreed with Royal Dutch/Shell in 1912. This was for the supply of crude oil and products and secured an outlet for Anglo-Persian's production.

With the Royal Dutch/Shell agreement in place Anglo-Persian was still anxious to secure additional capital and revenue. After lengthy negotiations, in 1914 a contract was signed with the Admiralty for the supply of boiler fuel oil. The Royal Navy was modernising its huge fleet and in addition to commissioning new warships it was converting existing ones from coal to oil firing. To guarantee supplies the government injected capital into Anglo-Persian in return for a majority shareholding. This also protected Anglo-Persian from domination by Royal Dutch/Shell. The government's shareholding in the company persisted until the 1980s when, apart from a small residual holding, it was finally disposed of in 1987.

During the First World War the British armed forces were Anglo-Persian's most

Left: Anglo-Persian acquired the British Petroleum Company Ltd in 1917. B.P. was originally the British subsidiary of a German company. This Bristol tanker dates from about the time of the B.P. take-over. It has a two compartment tank of probably no more than 500 gallons capacity. The lorry was restricted to a 12 mph speed limit and it is, of course, on solid tyres.

important customer, but the company was still keen to develop other business.

In 1917 it acquired a UK marketing organisation called the British Petroleum Company which was the British subsidiary of the German owned Europaische Petroleum Union. After the war Anglo-Persian acquired the Scottish shale oil industry - Scottish Oils - and expanded into Europe by buying or forming companies in most countries. In the 1920s Anglo-Persian opened its first British refineries: Llandarcy in South Wales in 1921 and Grangemouth in 1924. An Australian refinery was also constructed and exploration was extended to territories such as Canada, South America and

Africa. As a result of this expansion, by 1927 Anglo-Persian was one of the world's largest oil companies.

Having achieved world-wide prominence in the oil industry, Anglo-Persian faced difficulties in the depression years of the late 1920s and early

Above: A line-up of B.P. tankers in London circa 1920. Petrol was called motor spirit in those days and several aspects of tanker design, as specified by the Carriage of Petroleum Regulations, are apparent and are still relevant today. Note the fire screen separating the tank from the cab and the exhaust pipe mounted behind the front wheel, in this case as far forward as possible.

Right: No. 3684 in the B.P. fleet was this K5 Karrier fitted with a 1250 gallon single compartment fuel oil tank. The location is Burmah House, London in 1925, headquarters of the parent company.

This Dennis was the first motor lorry to enter service at the B.P. depot at Harrogate in 1920. The tank is probably a demountable type as several petrol cans are apparent. Interestingly all the tankers from this era had electric lights; the majority of contemporary lorries had oil lamps. Obviously naked flames and petrol tankers could result in serious problems.

Above: Anglo-Persian and Shell established a joint marketing and distribution company - Shell-Mex and B.P. Ltd - in 1932. This was to be a huge operation for the next 43 years. This AEC Majestic was new in 1934 and carries reference to Scottish Oils on the cab door. Anglo-Persian bought that bitumen producing company in 1920. The AEC's cab is very similar to the design used on contemporary Scammells.

1930s. To overcome these various problems several joint ventures were entered into, most notably with the Burmah Oil Company and Shell.

One of the most significant developments was the merger in 1932 between the marketing operations of Anglo-Persian and Shell. This was the formation of Shell-Mex and B.P. Anglo-Persian held a 40% stake and Shell the remaining 60%. Shell-Mex and B.P. was to become a major petrol and fuel retailer until it was dissolved in 1975 and also included brands such as National Benzole and Power.

The 1930s depression caused Anglo-Persian's profit to fall and this resulted in a reduction in royalty payments to the Persian government. Annoyed by this loss of revenue the Shah cancelled Anglo-Persian's concession in 1932. A new agreement was negotiated the following year and a period of recovery was enjoyed in the middle and late 1930s. The company was renamed the Anglo-Iranian Oil Company in 1935 and its interests were extended to other Middle Eastern states including Iraq and Kuwait.

The Second World War severely disrupted all of Anglo-Iranian's activities. The Shell-Mex and B.P. operation came under the control of the Pool Petroleum Board. Anglo-Iranian's large fleet of ocean going tankers was decimated and during the hostilities 657 crew members lost their lives.

The post-war reconstruction of Europe resulted in a period of expansion for Anglo-Iranian and by the late 1940s the company's Abadan refinery had become the largest in the world. Anglo-Iranian also ventured into petro-chemicals by jointly forming a company with Distillers Ltd. The progress of the late 1940s was interrupted in 1951 when the Iranian Government nationalised Anglo-Iranian's assets. These interests then were Britain's largest overseas investment and this action caused an international crisis. Anglo-Iranian's operations in Iran were halted. It took three years of intensive negotiations to resolve this crisis and a consortium of oil companies restarted the Iranian oil industry in 1954. Anglo-Iranian was renamed the British Petroleum Company Limited and it held a 40% share in the consortium.

The crisis in Iran had forced the company to broaden its horizons and crude oil production from other sources was increased. New refineries were built in Europe, Australia and Aden. In the 1950s exploration was carried out in the Persian Gulf, Canada, Europe, Africa and Australia.

Moving into the 1960s and expansion continued with oil production levels being steadily increased. BP extended its chemicals and petrochemicals interests in Great Britain and exploration in the North Sea commenced in 1965. Natural gas reserves were discovered first and in 1970 BP found oil in the famous Forties field which was the first major commercial oil discovery in the UK sector of the North Sea.

One year before this BP had discovered oil in Alaska at Prudhoe Bay. Such was the size of this latter oilfield that it was the biggest in the USA and BP as part owner decided to involve a major American oil company in its development. This led to an agreement with Standard Oil Company of Ohio which took over BP's leases in Alaska in return for BP obtaining 25% of Standard's equity. The BP stakeholding was so geared that it would become a majority shareholder in Standard once a certain production level was surpassed.

The decade of the 1970s was one of upheaval for the world-wide oil industry. BP was not immune from these traumas and the company lost access to most of its oil supplies from the OPEC countries. The Organisation of Petroleum Exporting Companies had been formed in 1960 and mainly represented Middle Eastern, African and Far Eastern oil producers.

By the 1970s OPEC was sufficiently well organised and influential enough to dictate world crude oil prices. The unprecedented price increase for crude oil resulted in much higher prices for refined products, this having a dramatic effect on demand for all producers including BP. As the decade drew to a close sales had recovered somewhat, but in 1979 BP suffered another blow when its Nigerian assets were nationalised.

By 1980 BP's investments in the North Sea and Alaska were able to offset the disruption in supplies of the previous years. BP diversified into other markets including feed milling and nutrition in the USA, household cleaning and industrial care products, minerals and coal mining and trading.

During the 1980s BP reduced its European refining capacity and pursued a more flexible crude oil buying policy. Traditionally it had bought its supplies on fixed, long term contracts but it changed to buying on the 'spot' markets. In 1987 BP successfully bid for the remainder of Standard Oil's shares, this company being renamed BP America.

By the late 1980s BP was pursuing a new policy of concentrating on its core hydro-carbon businesses and sold most of the subsidiaries it had acquired a few years earlier. Another large acquisition in this period was that of Britoil which was Government owned and concentrated on North Sea exploration and development. By the early 1990s BP was once again primarily a fully integrated oil company active in all

spheres of operations and it had retained its extensive petrochemicals and general chemicals interests.

With the dissolution of the Shell-Mex and B.P. marketing agreement in 1975 BP started to build its own retailing operation. It inherited the former National Benzole forecourts and started to procure its own service station sites. Within a few years the BP roadside image was very strong and this was consolidated in 1989 when the

company launched a campaign to present a stronger corporate style. The BP shield logo was redesigned and green became the dominant colour in tanker liveries and at service stations.

Since 1975 BP has pursued a policy of buying vehicles manufactured in Britain, these have included various Leyland, ERF and Seddon Atkinson models. During the 1990s ERF has become the predominant marque in the BP road tanker fleet.

Top: Armstrong Saurer was a joint venture between the Swiss company Saurer who were diesel engine pioneers, and Armstrong Whitworth of Newcastle upon Tyne. These vehicles were very well engineered, heavy and expensive. Production lasted for approximately five years from 1930 to 1935, and Shell-Mex and B.P. was one of the largest operators of the marque.

Above: This Dennis Max was supplied to the Pool Board in 1943. It has a wartime utility cab and passed to Shell-Mex and B.P. after the dissolution of the Pool Board in 1948. Note the logo with B.P. incorporated into the Shell.

Above: Drawbar tanker and trailer operations have never been common in this country. AEC Mammoth Major Eight Mk.III, registration number MLC573 new in the early 1950s and with a two compartment fuel oil tank is pulling a single compartment tank trailer. The trailer is a frameless design with the weight carried directly by the axles, and the drawbar appears to be very long by the standards of the time.

Left: Full reference to both oil companies was made in the tanker liveries used for the duration of Shell-Mex and B.P. This is a Thornycroft eight wheeler fuel oil tanker dating from the late 1950s, and painted in the dark green and red paint scheme. The cab was designed and made by Alfred Miles and would certainly never win any awards for attractiveness.

Right: AEC Mammoth Major eight wheelers were used in quantity by Shell-Mex and B.P. This Mk.III version has a six compartment 4000 gallon tank. The distinctive sliding door style of cab with protruding headlights was made by Reeve and Kenning.

Above: A photograph from a more unusual angle, it being taken over a Leyland Octopus 24.04 eight wheeler at Fulham Terminal. Note the dip-sticks on top of the tanker and lamp for the driver. The diversity of lorries in the background illustrates the many makes in the Shell-Mex and B.P. fleet: Scammells, Leylands, Albion, AEC and Dennis.

Right: When Shell-Mex and B.P. terminated their long-standing agreement in 1975, the National Benzole name and service stations passed to BP. All forecourts were soon changed to the BP format, but the National Benzole name was re-introduced for a short period in the early 1980s when the oil industry was being investigated by the Monopolies Commission. This Seddon Atkinson eight wheeler was new in 1981 and it is carrying National livery.

Right: After the dissolution of Shell-Mex and B.P. Ltd in 1975 both former partners pursued their own policies for transport and distribution. BP have purchased mainly British built makes, this Seddon Atkinson tractor unit entered service in 1984.

Below: The ERF marque has a strong presence in the modern BP fleet and this E14 model entered service in 1989. It is a rear-steer six wheel tractor unit coupled to a tandem axle semi-trailer. This scenic photograph was taken in the Trossachs.

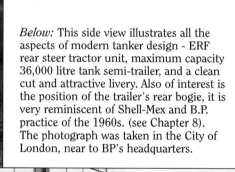

Below: This side view illustrates all the aspects of modern tanker design - ERF rear steer tractor unit, maximum capacity 36,000 litre tank semi-trailer, and a clean cut and attractive livery. Also of interest is the position of the trailer's rear bogie, it is very reminiscent of Shell-Mex and B.P. practice of the 1960s. (see Chapter 8). The photograph was taken in the City of London, near to BP's headquarters.

FOOTNOTE

Whilst this book was in preparation it was announced on 29 February 1996 that BP and Mobil had agreed to a joint venture by merging their European refining and marketing operations. This agreement will operate in 43 countries (subject to ratification by various regulatory bodies). For the petrol retailing part of the merger BP will hold 70% of the equity and Mobil the remainder. BP will have operational control of the assets.

Conoco Limited (Jet Petroleum)

In addition to the fully integrated oil companies active in Great Britain for many decades, there have also been several fuel distributors and retailers which have built substantial sales volumes by purchasing bulk supplies from the major oil refiners. Many of these have been, and indeed still are, regional companies with a strong presence in a certain geographical area. Initially Jet Petroleum was such a retailer, but it expanded rapidly throughout the country and was taken over by the Continental Oil Company, a long established American oil producer better known as Conoco, in 1961.

The decade of the 1950s was notable for the arrival of several new petrol brands. Some were natural progressions from established companies such as Mobil; others were entrepreneurial ventures aimed at capturing a share of a rapidly growing market. Jet Petroleum was in the latter category and was founded in 1953 by Robert Hanson and some of his business associates in Huddersfield. Robert Hanson was chairman of Hanson and Holdsworth, a large and famous road haulage company which had been nationalised in 1948. After de-nationalisation in 1953 Hanson Transport was reformed and incorporated several other interests. Amongst these was Bottomleys Motors (later Yorkshire Car Hire) which provided wedding and funeral limousines, taxis, car hire and also operated petrol filling stations. These became the first forecourts to retail the Jet brand.

The established petroleum producers and retailers were keen to protect their businesses so some newcomers, and Jet was one, cut prices to attract customers. Indeed, Jet claimed to be the first cut-price brand in the country. Trading stamps were also another means of tempting motorists to change to a different petrol.

Jet bought supplies from several sources including Regent Oil. It soon established depots and terminals and built up national coverage, supported by strong advertising and marketing.

In the 1950s it was still common for family owned service stations to offer more than one brand of petrol, although the solus trading concept was rapidly gaining in popularity. During its formative years Jet targeted smaller garages and multi-brand outlets in addition to winning contracts with bulk purchasers such as bus companies and hauliers. By 1961, Jet, still under Robert Hanson's chairmanship, was expanding at the rate of one new depot every year. It had facilities at Immingham, Ellesmere Port, Cardiff, Cliffe (Medway), Plymouth and Felixstowe. Coastal tankers supplied Felixstowe and road tankers transferred petrol and diesel fuel from there to other terminals such as Cliffe and Immingham.

The Continental Oil Company - Conoco - is one of the oldest in the oil industry. It was founded in 1875 as the Continental Oil and Transportation Company based at Ogden in the state of Utah, although it was actually

incorporated at Council Bluffs, Iowa. The founder and major shareholder, Isaac E Blake, had started trading in crude oil some years previously and he made and lost one fortune before forming Conoco. In 1879 Isaac E Blake was instrumental in forming the Pacific Coast Oil Company in California, to which Chevron can trace its origins. Conoco grew into a fully integrated oil company and in 1961 bought Jet

Petroleum. Initially it tried to promote its own brand image in this country, but such was the strength and popularity of Jet, the established name continued. For several years road tankers were liveried Conoco and Jet, but today the Jet brand prevails. Conoco has built the Jet name over the years and the brand has been introduced into Europe and new markets in the Far East.

Back to the 1960s, and Conoco

Above: When Jet Petroleum was founded in 1953 the tanker fleet was mainly based on AEC models. Two Mammoth Major Mk.III eight wheelers carrying personalised 'JET' registration numbers are shown; the vehicles dating back to the formation of the company.

announced plans to build a refinery here, its first such venture outside the USA. In 1969 the Conoco/Jet refinery at Killingholme on Humberside came into production. North Sea exploration commenced and was rewarded with crude oil discoveries in the 1970s. Today Conoco is owned by the giant DuPont Corporation and is active in all sectors of the British oil and petroleum industry.

At the formation of Jet Petroleum, the road tanker fleet consisted of vehicles almost entirely of AEC manufacture. The AEC Mammoth Major Eight Mk.III was the prominent model and later in the 1950s AEC Mercurys and Mammoth Major Mk.Vs were also purchased. A few Atkinson eight wheelers were also acquired. Hanson and Holdsworth had bought a majority interest in Oswald Tillotson in 1935, and Tillotsons became a large and well known AEC dealer and distributor; hence the strong AEC connection with Jet in the 1950s and 60s.

This same vehicle buying policy continued after Conoco acquired Jet Petroleum until the AECs were replaced by other Leyland Group models after the demise of the Southall built marque. DAF, and later Leyland-DAF lorries were used during the late 1970s and 80s.

Today, in addition to DAFs, Volvo and ERF vehicles also feature in the Conoco/Jet fleet which is still operated by the company.

Top: A 'tin-front' cabbed AEC Mammoth Major Mk.III eight wheeler with a two compartment tank delivering diesel fuel to a large bus operator. The Jet motif was based on a profile of a delta-winged aeroplane, a revolutionary design in the 1950s.

Above right: AEC Mercury medium weight lorries complemented the heavy weight Mammoth Majors in the Jet fleet. This late 1950s model, with a longer than usual wheelbase for a four wheeled tanker, has a five compartment tank. Capacity was 2700 gallons of petrol; less if diesel, or if a mixed petrol and diesel load was being carried.

Right: Side view of one of the Atkinson eight wheelers operated by Jet. This is a five compartment tank of 4000 gallons capacity. Most unusually Jet mounted the lorry's own fuel tank on the nearside of the chassis along with the tank discharge valves. By the time this vehicle entered service most tankers had their fuel tanks mounted on the off-side of the chassis.

Above: This AEC Mammoth Major Mk V eight wheel tanker is seen making a delivery to a customer's premises in the early 1960's. The driver is in the process of checking the tank contents with a calibrated dip-stick. The vehicle, designed to operate at 24 tons gvw, is fitted with a five compartment 4000 gallon tank.

Left: When Conoco built its refinery at Killingholme on Humberside in the mid 1960s this memorial was re-located. It had first been erected by the Anglo-American Society of Hull in 1924 to commemorate the voyage of the Pilgrim Fathers to Holland in 1609, from where they journeyed to Plymouth Rock in America in 1620. Posing alongside are an AEC Mercury and an AEC Mammoth Major Mk.V eight wheeler.

Conoco Limited (Jet Petroleum)

Left: Revised Conoco livery, predominantly light brown and white, which was introduced in the 1970s. The lorry is a Seddon Atkinson 301 six wheeler from the late 1970s operated by South East Coast Oil Services Ltd.

Right: For a period of approximately 20 years until legislation changes in the 1960s, the rigid eight wheeler was the flagship of many of the oil companies' fleets. Nowadays they are not very common, but this DAF 2500 eight wheeler maintained the tradition into the 1990s. It was new in 1987/8.

Below: Volvo F6S four wheeler operated by Mersey Oil Co Ltd of Southport. The tanker was new in 1983/4 and has hose reel equipment for making deliveries to houses and other small usage customers. Tank capacity is 2500 gallons.

Conoco Limited (Jet Petroleum)

Below: The latest Jet livery of yellow and blue. The lorry is a DAF 2100 six wheeler with a five compartments tank of 3600 gallons (16,000 litres). It also has hose reel equipment.

Above: DAF 2500 tractor unit new in 1987/8 with LPG tanker semi-trailer. Note both Jet and Conoco names in the livery.

Right: In the 1990s the Conoco/Jet fleet consists of chassis from several of the leading commercial vehicle manufacturers. This Volvo FL10 rear steer six wheel tractor unit was new in 1992 and it is coupled to a six compartment tandem-axle tank semi-trailer.

Above: Not all articulated vehicles operate at the 38 tonnes gross train weight limit and this four axle outfit is restricted to 32.512 tonnes gtw. This DAF 2700 ATI was new in 1992 and typically the tank capacity is 29,000 litres (6400 gallons).

Left: The Leyland-DAF 80 series utilised an up-dated version of the Leyland T45 Roadtrain cab, originally introduced in 1980. This DAF engined tractor unit was new in 1991/2 and is seen outside of the Conoco offices at Warwick.

Esso UK plc

The Anglo-American Oil Company was established in 1888 to import lamp oil from its American parent company. Anglo-American was the first foreign affiliate of The Standard Oil Trust whose origins dated back to 1870 when John D. Rockefeller set up the Standard Oil Company of Ohio. Later, in 1911, the trust was dissolved on the orders of the United States Government into thirty four unrelated companies. One of these, Standard Oil (New Jersey) then acquired Anglo-American.

Initially all the supplies of lamp oil were imported into a storage wharf at Purfleet and the three grades of oil retailed were soon selling in large quantities. As the first 'horseless carriages' ventured hesitantly on to the roads, Pratts Petrol was imported from 1896 to satisfy a new demand. Charles Pratt had been one of the founder members of Standard Oil.

Motor Spirit, or petrol, soon became an important product for Anglo-American and as early as 1905 they had constructed an experimental road-going petrol tanker. The steel tank was of 800 gallons capacity and was mounted on a Thornycroft lorry chassis capable of travelling at 8 mph. Petrol was usually sold to motorists in 2 gallons cans from a diverse variety of outlets ranging from blacksmiths, ironmongers and even chemists' shops. In 1919 Anglo-American introduced the first kerbside pump in the United Kingdom at a garage in Hale, Cheshire.

In the first half of the twentieth century paraffin sales were very important for all oil companies. Anglo-American was no exception and in 1920 they bought the Valor Company, which in addition to manufacturing paraffin heaters also sold large numbers of cooking ranges. These cookers and ovens were acceptable alternatives to town gas appliances in many homes, particularly in rural communities.

Anglo-American continued to expand rapidly during the 1920s and new importing terminals were opened at Hull, Avonmouth and Ellesmere Port. The company opened its first service station at Harrow Road, Paddington in 1921 and it offered a 24 hours service.

In 1925 Anglo-American bought the British Mexican Petroleum Co. Ltd whose main brand was Redline petrol. A couple of years previously Brit-Mex had acquired the Atlantic Gulf and West Indies Oil Company, along with their small refinery at Fawley. A further take-over for Anglo-American in 1927 was that of the Glico Petroleum Company. One year later Pratts 'Ethyl' petrol was introduced containing tetra-ethyl lead as an anti-knocking agent. By 1932

Anglo-American claimed that this brand was on sale at 1800 retail pumps throughout the country, and in the same year the last horse retired from their huge distribution fleet.

The Esso brand name was introduced into the UK in 1934, some eight years after being used for the first time in the USA. It was the phonetic pronunciation of S O - Standard Oil's initials, and in 1935 all the brands of petrol were changed to Esso. The Pratts name however, continued to be used for some lubricants until the 1950s.

Anglo-American Oil acquired a controlling interest in the Cleveland Petroleum Company Ltd in 1938, and in September 1939 on the formation of the Petroleum and Lubricating Oil Boards, Anglo-American's activities came under the Government controlled pooling arrangements.

After the Second World War Anglo-American continued its growth and expansion and in 1949 construction of a new refinery started at Fawley. The period of war between 1939-45 had highlighted how desperately short of refining capacity Great Britain was in times of national emergency. The post war years when there was a shortage of dollars for the purchase of crude oil and refined products prompted Anglo-American and other oil companies to construct new refineries. Not only did these new facilities provide some much needed additional capacity, they were also designed to process Middle Eastern crude oil which could be purchased with pounds sterling.

In 1951 Anglo-American changed its name to the Esso Petroleum Company Limited and later in that year Fawley refinery came into production. The 1950s decade was a notable one for Esso with huge increases in petrol sales being recorded.

By 1960 petrol sales volumes had trebled in comparison to the levels of some ten years previously. This had been achieved through a policy of convincing retailers of the benefits of solus trading. This was also backed up by Esso's Dealer Co-operation Plan which included full support and technical service from the company along with training for forecourt staff and retailers. Fawley refinery provided Esso with the means to be virtually self-sufficient in this country and as it was developed in the 1950s, Esso Blue paraffin and Esso Green tractor vapourising oil were just two additional brands which were introduced.

The large increase in sales volumes recorded by Esso resulted in another refinery being opened at Milford Haven in 1960. This was designed to produce fuel oil and middle distillates such as paraffin, diesel and jet engine fuel. In the early 1960s the steel industry and the Central Electricity Generating Board were very large users of fuel oil, low world crude oil prices encouraging the movement away from coal fired power station boilers to oil burning on a massive scale.

In 1962 Esso discontinued their Redline and Glico petrol brands, and in 1963 exploration surveys commenced in the North Sea. They were carried out in a joint venture with Shell and the first crude oil was brought on shore in 1976. Esso and Shell still work in partnership in the North Sea oil and gas fields.

After a twenty years period of spectacular growth Esso and the oil industry suffered the effects of the world oil crisis of 1973. Massive price rises for crude oil led to large reductions in demand and within two years sales had fallen by 20%. The economic recession of the early 1980s caused a further drop in demand by 10%. The largest casualty was the fuel oil market with a huge fall in industrial consumption. Esso was a major supplier to both the steel industry and the electricity generators and the sharp decline in sales they experienced caused some complications for the company. Some refinery units had to be taken out of commission and in 1983 the Milford Haven refinery was closed. Some distribution terminals were also closed and surplus road tankers disposed of. After taking painful and difficult decisions Esso emerged from this very traumatic period a leaner and stronger company.

The parent Standard Oil Company (New Jersey) changed its name to the Exxon Corporation in June 1972,

Top: After the First World War horses became very expensive because of the huge losses caused by the conflict. Motor vehicles started to replace them in large numbers and this one, possibly an imported White, was bodied by Hayes of Stamford in 1918. It was used for carrying 2 gallons cans of petrol. Chain drive, solid tyres, acetylene lamps and note the bulb horn and fire extinguisher.

Above: One of the imported American makes, a USA 'Liberty' dating from 1918. It has a two compartment tank with an estimated capacity of 800 gallons. Note the ornate Royal Warrant on the side of the cab.

although the name Esso continued in usage in this country. In 1973 the Cleveland service stations were integrated into the Esso chain.

Moving into the 1980s and Fawley refinery continued to be uprated and modernised so that today it is the largest refinery in the UK and processes crude oil mainly sourced from the North Sea. Much of its production is supplied to regional terminals, depots and even the major airports via a pipeline network.

As Esso approached its centenary of operations in Great Britain in 1988 its activities were characterised by a further and sustained period of modernisation, expansion and improvement in all spheres of operations. Today, in the mid 1990s Esso is one of Britain's largest fully integrated oil companies and has a major presence in all aspects of the industry.

Firstly as Anglo-American and later as Esso, the company has operated huge numbers of vehicles. The scale of its operations can be gauged by the statistics for 1920. Then it had established a national sales and supply network of over 700 inland depots. By 1926 Anglo-American operated 2700 motor lorries in addition to having a large number of horses. During the early 1930s Anglo-American rationalised its distribution activities and many depots were closed,

This Foden overtype steam wagon was based at Vauxhall Road depot, Liverpool and was used specifically for lubricating oils deliveries. It was photographed in 1920 when it had been in service for several years. Obviously steamers were unsuitable for carrying lighter distillates.

consequently the number of lorries fell by half and the last horses retired.

After the second world war and during the 1950s Esso used larger road tankers to distribute its products. As service stations changed to solus trading, bigger storage tanks were installed resulting in greater quantities of petrol being delivered. By the end of the 1950s such was Esso's market penetration that it started to appoint a network of authorised distributors to handle sales to agricultural, domestic and smaller industrial users.

In the early 1960s Esso constructed its first pipeline from Fawley to its west London depot, and now all its major terminals are supplied in this way obviating the need for large quantities of products to be transported by rail or road.

Over the years Esso has bought many different makes of lorry and examples of all the well known British built types have been operated at some period. For many years Leyland, Scammell and AEC models were used in quantity. These were augmented in the 1950s and 1960s with ERFs and Fodens amongst others. By the mid 1980s the favoured makes were ERF, Foden and Seddon Atkinson. These particular makes of lorry still feature in the Esso fleet which delivers petrol and diesel fuel to its service stations. Deliveries to other large users of fuels are normally handled by contract hauliers.

Above: The Esso brand name was introduced into this country in 1934 and all Anglo-American's petrol brands were marketed under the new name from the following year. This solid tyred Scammell six wheeler articulated lorry pre-dates the name change by several years but it was repainted to reflect the new branding.

Left: By the mid 1920s Anglo-American was operating a fleet of over 2500 motor vehicles. In 1926 the General Strike caused serious difficulties and after a few days essential convoys were organised. This is one such operation and some of these in London received escort by armoured cars.

Top right: Cleveland Petroleum came under the control of Anglo-American in 1938. After the re-introduction of company brands in the early 1950s Cleveland continued to be marketed separately from Esso. This 1950 Leyland Beaver has a four compartment tank. Note that a 'Cleveland' badge adorns the front grille in place of 'Leyland'. It was photographed in Halifax in 1960.

Above right: A typical Esso articulated road tanker of the 1950s. The five compartment Carrimore semi-trailer tank, coupled to a Bedford 'SA' tractor unit, was designed to carry 2400 gallons of petroleum spirit.

Right: A 1954 Scammell 'Artic Eight' with a permanently coupled insulated Scammell two-compartment tank trailer designed to carry 3250 gallons of fuel oil.

A 1952 Leyland Octopus 22.0/1
fitted with an elliptical six-
compartment 3600 gallon spirit
tank. In production from 1947 to
1954, the model was powered by
Leyland's O.600 9.8 litre diesel
engine developing 125 bhp and was
designed to operate at 22 tons gvw.

O PETROLEUM COMPANY, LTD.

Right: Bedford S type articulated tanker at Preston terminal in 1960. The Cleveland livery still retained the term 'Motor Spirit' although by that time the product was universally referred to as petrol. The Bedford was one of the last of its type to enter service, being replaced by the new TK range in 1960.

Below: Esso operated a mixed fleet and some ERF tractor units were bought in the 1960s. This 6LV/L cabbed model is prominent in this view alongside an Atkinson Mk.1 articulated outfit operated by Dobson of Edinburgh on contract to Esso. By the mid 1960s Esso had changed its livery to a predominantly white style.

Left: Aircraft refuelling services have resulted in many special vehicles being designed for usage solely within the confines of airports. This is a Foden eight wheeler articulated bowser dating from the early 1960s. It is refuelling a Boeing 707 operated by the German airline, Lufthansa.

A Century of Petroleum Transport

Left: A Foden S20 aircraft refueller, fleet no. T3186, at Birmingham Airport servicing a BEA Trident in February 1970; note the observation windows high in the unit's cab, very much a necessity when manoeuvring such large vehicles on an airport's ramp close to aircraft wings or fuselages.

Below: Esso operated a sizeable fleet of Bedford TK artics in the early 1960s, with three clearly visible in this depot view. They were normally operated with four or five compartments tank semi-trailers of up to 3000 gallons capacity. In the background is a Dennis four wheeler owned by an authorised Esso distributor.

Below: Esso continued to buy British into the 1970s and AEC Mandators replaced their Leyland Beavers. British Leyland, of which AEC was a member, had wanted to phase out the Mandator in favour of their Buffalo and Marathon, but the reliability of the Mandator and repeat orders from several oil companies ensured that it remained in production until 1977. This Mandator was new in 1975.

Above: By the late 1960s Leyland Beavers were very prominent in Esso's fleet. This fine view shows an unusual eight compartment 6000 gallons tank semi-trailer. Note that the livery of this period incorporated the Cleveland brand name as well as Esso. The reliable tilt-cab Beaver had a relatively short production life from 1965 to 1971, when it was replaced by the troublesome Buffalo.

Right: Leyland Beaver tractor unit which entered service in 1968 with a tandem axle fuel oil semi-trailer. Esso had a huge amount of business in the heavy oil market at the time and this single compartment insulated tank transported the commodity hot, for easy discharge at its destination. Because of its high viscosity heavy fuel oil is sold by weight and not volume.

Left: A more conventional aircraft refueller based on a 1986 Volvo FL10 tractor unit and tandem axle semi-trailer. The specialist pumps and filters are housed in the rear compartment of the tanker. Note the Exxon logo, the parent company of Esso.

Left below: In 1983 the maximum gross train weight was raised from 32.5 to 38 tonnes. An extra axle was required to meet the new limits resulting in a variety of combinations of two axle tractor plus tri-axle semi-trailer, or three axle tractor and tandem axle trailer. This 2+3 combination of ERF C40 tractor and tri-axle 35,000 litre semi-trailer was new in 1983. By this time litres had replaced gallons for measurement.

Below: Deliveries are made to all kinds of locations and construction projects, open-cast coal mining sites and quarries, etc. All require gas oil to fuel plant and off-road vehicles. This authorised distributor's Foden eight wheeler is making such a delivery. The storage tank is a 1951 AEC six wheeler, new to the Ministry of Defence as an airfield bowser.

FINA plc

In February 1920 the Compagnie Financiere Belge des Petroles - Petrofina - was founded by a group of investors in Antwerp. Its first venture was to explore for, extract and refine petroleum products in Romania through the Concordia company. However, before the Romanian exploration could be started Petrofina and Pure Oil of Delaware established Purfina in May 1920 and this was for the distribution of oil and petrol in Belgium and Holland.

By 1923 Petrofina had taken full ownership of Purfina and in the same year the purchase of a small refinery at Ertvelde allowed the company to expand into the lubricating oil market. Sales of paraffin were a large and important part of Petrofina's business and it was sold in glass bottles through many outlets including grocery shops.

The origins of Petrofina (UK) can be traced back to 1927 and the founding of the Cities Service Oil Company. This was the British subsidiary of an American concern and the Petrofina Group bought this company in 1939.

On the outbreak of war, in the September of that year, Fina was included in the pooling arrangements of the government organised Petroleum Board.

From 1948 onwards Fina started to expand rapidly in this country by recruiting service station owners for solus trading and it increased its depot network across the UK. The parent company, in a joint venture with other partners, built a new refinery in Antwerp and this came into production in 1951. At that time most of the crude oil came from the African continent. Later on in the 1950s exploration was successful in Mexico and Canada with the discovery of large crude oil reserves.

The 1950s was a decade which saw rapid expansion for Petrofina world-wide, and in Great Britain there was a growing market for Fina petrol and diesel fuels. Expansion continued in the 1960s and Fina established aircraft refuelling services at several British airports including Heathrow. Large scale exploration under the North Sea commenced in 1965 with natural gas being discovered the following year. In 1968 Lindsey Oil Refinery was opened on Humberside in partnership with Total. The refinery made a significant impact on Fina's UK operations by providing it with a dedicated source of refined products.

Fina located substantial crude oil reserves as a partner in the Ekofisk oilfield off the Norwegian coast. The first oil from the UK sector of the North Sea was pumped into Fina's tanks at Lindsey in September 1971.

The revenue generated from Ekofisk had a major impact on the Petrofina Group's finances and helped the company, and its subsidiary Fina, to expand dramatically in the 1970s. This growth was not confined to Europe but extended to North America also. Into the 1980s and Petrofina was firmly established as a large international oil company. In 1988 it became the sole owner of the Antwerp refinery.

In Britain Fina constructed Fina-Line which was a £50 million-plus investment, and is a 139 miles long underground pipeline which runs from Lindsey Oil Refinery to its terminal at Buncefield, Hertfordshire. Since being completed in 1990 Fina-Line has greatly improved Fina's logistics and supply of petrol, derv and kerosene into the major markets of south eastern England.

Today, Petrofina and the British subsidiary Fina plc are fully integrated oil companies. They are involved in all aspects of the business including exploration and production, refining, and retailing. Fina in Great Britain operates its own service stations in addition to supplying independently operated sites.

Until September 1995 Fina operated its own fleet of road tankers and directly employed the drivers. Since then employment and management of the tanker drivers has been contracted out.

From its first days in this country Fina used several makes of lorries. Leylands and Bedford were prominent during 1939 and in the period following the Second World War the Fina fleet comprised mainly of former Pool Petroleum tankers. These were of Dennis, Bedford and Maudslay manufacture.

During the 1950s Bedfords were again the most common smaller lorries and the Leyland Octopus and AEC Mammoth Major Eight Mk.III models were the usual larger tankers. Towards the end of the decade Atkinson eight wheelers also featured strongly.

Come the 1960s and AEC, Leyland and Atkinson became the core marques in the Fina fleet. By the 1970s Leyland Group vehicles were the most

Above: This delightful photograph dates from the late 1940s and was taken at Grangemouth terminal. It was obviously posed because everyone is busy doing something! The vehicles are interesting; a Morris Commercial Leader which was a model from before the War, and a Bedford O-type with a utility bonnet and grille, this denoting its manufacture as being during the 1939-45 war years.

Left: Peterborough Depot, April 1949. A pair of Bedford WH lorries dating from the mid 1930s. The one nearest the camera has a two-compartment tank with a capacity of probably 1000 gallons. The other Bedford is larger with a three-compartment tank of probably 1500 gallons capacity. The personnel are identified as, left to right, B J Waghorn, S J Barton (Superintendent), D G W Petch and L W Wright.

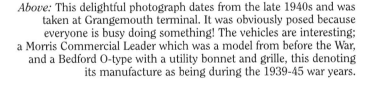

Left: After the dissolution of the Pool Petroleum Board in 1948, many of the tankers were disposed of to individual companies. This International was one of many 'lease-lend' lorries which arrived during the war years for service in the Pool fleet. It has a four-compartment tank and the photograph was taken at Leeds in July 1949.

Above: Maudslay of Coventry built a large quantity of their Mogul four wheelers for the Pool Petroleum Board during the war and in the period immediately afterwards. These Mogul Mk.II lorries are probably from the post-war batch and were passed to Fina in late 1948. The majority of these were powered by AEC 7.7 litre engines, the remainder being fitted with Gardner 5LW units. These two examples have three-compartment, 1500 gallon tanks and the location is Gunness terminal, Lincolnshire.

Right: All the oil companies operate a variety of vehicles for various tasks. This O-type Bedford carried a small tank for deliveries of lubricating oil in bulk and had sufficient space in the body for drums of lubricants.

prominent, until by 1977 when the road tanker fleet was 220 strong and 100% Leyland, including a few AECs. That company of course was part of the Leyland empire.

This domination lasted into the early 1980s when examples of the Seddon Atkinson marque began operating alongside Leyland T45 Roadtrains, whilst in the 1990s the latest additions to enter the Fina fleet are Mercedes tractor units.

Right: By the mid 1950s Fina was operating larger and heavier lorries as business expanded. This Leyland Octopus 22.0/1 eight wheeler carried a six-compartment tank of 3600 gallons capacity.

Above: Fina opened a new depot at Sheffield in the early 1950s and the first tanker to be loaded was duly photographed. this was a Morris Commercial and the vehicle carried quite a large tank for a lightweight chassis. It was a four compartment type, probably of 1800 gallons capacity. The men on the tanker are identified as B. Corbett and W. Glossop. Note the Petrol pump for internal use.

Thornycroft supplied a number of Trusty eight wheelers to the Pool Petroleum Board, this particular model remaining in production until 1957. Fina operated the example illustrated here, with a twin compartment tank of 3000 gallons capacity, for the delivery of diesel and gas oil. It is believed to be one of the tankers that originally saw service with the post war Pool Petroleum Board.

Above: Two Fina drivers exchange pleasantries as a Bulwark contract vehicle leaves the terminal and an AEC Mammoth Major waits to load at the rack. In common with Bulwark policy, the Atkinson, fleet no. 178 and dating from 1954, features a lightweight Duramin cab.

Left: Although the Fina shields on this tanker have been retouched for some reason, the photograph is included because it shows an interesting vehicle. The Dodge Kew model was not particularly common as an articulated tractor unit and this one is coupled to an unusual design of semi-trailer. The tank was specifically built for lubricating oil with a large front compartment and four smaller ones in the rear section.

Left: This Dodge 300-series four wheeler dates from 1959. The 'LAD' cab fitted to these models was a design shared with Leyland and Albion. The vehicle features a four-compartment tank of 1500 gallons capacity. Note the trade plates left lying on the grass in the right-hand foreground of this official photograph.

Below: A typical maximum weight fuel oil tanker from the early 1950s. The tank on this Duramin-cabbed AEC Mammoth Major Mk.III eight wheeler appears to be of a three-compartment design.

Left: Atkinson introduced a revised model in the late 1950s featuring a new coachbuilt cab and detailed chassis improvements. This attractive example from the early 1960s carries a square profile tank very well. Even though it was fitted with a Gardner 6LX '150' engine, the vehicle was still modestly powered for operating at 24 tons gross weight.

FINA plc

Left: Even though Fina's Stourport on Severn depot was flooded in January and February 1960, deliveries to customers still had to be made. An Austin 7-tonner and Bedford S-type are seen loading in the flood waters.

Above: This Atkinson tractor unit was new in 1964 and it is coupled to an insulated tank semi-trailer. Such tankers were, and are, used for carrying heavy or 'black' fuel oils as used in power stations and similar boiler installations. Typically '950 seconds' oil is sold by weight and not volume because it is so thick. It has to be transported hot so that it can be pumped out at its destination. When new and operating to the weight limits of 1964, the payload of this tanker would have been approximately 15 tons.

Left: The mid 1960s saw a change of livery for Fina and this AEC Mandator with a six-compartment tank semi-trailer was photographed in central London. The AEC was new in 1966 and recently introduced legislation gave it a significant advantage in payload over a rigid eight wheeler tanker. This hastened a switch to articulation, not only by the oil companies but by hauliers generally.

Above left: AEC Mammoth Major Mk.V eight wheeler in a fuel oils livery. At this date, in the early 1960s, Fina still depended mainly on rigid eights for their maximum weight operations.

Above: The mid and late 1960s was a period of vehicle rationalisation for Fina, with AECs and Leylands becoming the predominant makes. Although they were part of the same group and shared a common style of cab, the chassis and drive-lines were completely different. Here a 1969 AEC Mercury is seen delivering domestic heating oil.

Left: Another change of livery occurred in the mid 1970s with white and grey being the main colours. This Albion Clydesdale four wheeler with hose reel equipment, belonging to West Midland Fuels Ltd, presents a clean and attractive image.

FINA plc

Left: A 1973 Leyland Buffalo tractor unit and 6000 gallons capacity six-compartment tank semi-trailer. Note that the trailer is riding on super-single tyres.

Right: This Leyland Bison six wheeler was one of 36 similar examples ordered in 1976 and, along with 37 Leyland Buffalos, it brought the number of Leylands in the Fina fleet to 220.

Below: By the early 1980s Seddon Atkinsons were being bought by Fina. These two 401 tractor units entered service in 1982 and were powered by Rolls Royce Eagle engines. The six-compartment tank semi-trailers each having a capacity of 30,000 litres (6600 gallons).

Right: In the late 1980s there was a subtle change to the Fina livery with extended stripes on the tanks. This Seddon Atkinson Strato tractor unit entered service in 1989, and is coupled to a tri-axle semi-trailer of six compartments and 36,000 litres capacity (7900 gallons). The trailer is specially designed for a low height and therefore low centre of gravity in the interests of improved stability.

Right: The Leyland marque was still represented in the Fina fleet in the mid 1980s. This 1986 Leyland Roadtrain is pulling a conventional tri-axle semi-trailer of 36,000 litres capacity (7900 gallons) for operations at 38 tonnes gross train weight.

Below: A new livery was introduced in 1994 incorporating 'Fina Services' into the scheme to complement Fina service station design and colours. These two Mercedes 1834 articulated tankers highlight the effectiveness of this completely revised livery.

Gulf Oil (Chevron)

In 1996 Gulf Oil celebrated its centenary of business in Great Britain. Although US-owned for two thirds of that period, its origins date back to 1896 and the Mineral Oils Corporation Ltd of Silvertown, east London.

This company was established to refine Russian crude oil and manufacture lubricants. By 1901 a bulk storage depot had been opened in South Wales but the firm struggled financially and went into voluntary liquidation. However the business had potential and was sold as a going concern by the Receiver. The name was changed to the Silvertown Oil Storage Company and later to Silvertown Lubricants. After this uncertain start, the company prospered obtaining orders from large users of oils and grease such as railway companies, shipping lines and industrial concerns. It also tendered successfully for several British Government contracts. Regular and large exports were won in markets such as India, Egypt, South America and other developing countries. In 1928 the Gulf Oil Corporation of Pittsburgh, USA, bought Silvertown Lubricants and provided it with additional technical resources.

Gulf was founded as a result of an oil discovery in Texas in 1901. A refinery was constructed at Port Arthur and by 1912 the company's growth was such that a second Texas refinery was opened at Fort Worth. Gulf expanded rapidly and by 1928 it was one of America's major fully integrated oil companies.

With the commencement of hostilities in 1939, Gulf's British subsidiary became part of the Lubricating Oil Board and supplied aircraft engine oil to the RAF.

The Silvertown site continued to develop in the 1950s and Gulf's main European lubricants laboratory was situated there. In 1960 the parent company decided to expand its European activities and commenced marketing petrol and other fuels. Construction of a new refinery started at Milford Haven in the mid 1960s, coming into production in 1968. During the same period distribution terminals were opened throughout the UK to enable Gulf to service its growing customer base.

The 1970s saw Gulf steadily increase its petrol and fuels sales and acquiring service station sites. However, in this period, the parent company disposed of most of its European marketing and refining interests but maintained its commitment to the British market.

In 1984 the biggest merger in corporate history (at that time) was announced when the Chevron Corporation of San Francisco bought the Gulf Oil Corporation including the British subsidiary.

Chevron's origins dated back to 1879 when an oil discovery north of Los Angeles caused the formation of the Pacific Coast Oil Company.

In 1900 John D. Rockefeller's Standard Oil (New Jersey) bought Pacific Coast and constructed a refinery at Richmond, California. When the United States Government ordered the dissolution of the Standard Oil Trust in 1911, the Standard Oil Company (California) emerged as one of the 34 separate concerns. By the 1920s this company had become the largest producer of crude oil in the USA. Also at this time, Standard (California) merged with the Pacific Oil Company to form the Standard Oil Company of California (SOCAL). Photographs of the company's service stations taken in the USA in the 1920s and 30s show the Chevron logo prominently displayed, although it was not until 1977 that the company became known as Chevron USA Inc.

Chevron's origins in Great Britain can be traced to 1954 when Irancal was based in London to manage SOCAL's interests in the Iranian Consortium (see BP chapter). In 1964 SOCAL, in partnership with the Regent Oil Company commenced exploration in the North Sea and drilled the first well in the UK sector. There had been strong connections between these two companies since 1936 and the formation of Caltex by SOCAL and the Texas Oil Company. Caltex provided an outlet for SOCAL's Middle Eastern crude oil reserves through Texaco outlets in Europe, Africa and Asia.

Between 1968 and the 1984 merger with Gulf, Chevron Oil (UK) Ltd operated a network of service stations under the Chevron brand name in Great Britain. Approximately 100 of these being obtained from Regent in 1968 when Texaco assumed complete control of Regent. By the mid 1970s, the Chevron retailing chain had doubled in size but immediately prior to the 1984 merger Texaco bought all the Chevron service stations.

Gulf Oil and its parent Chevron operate together in Great Britain as a fully integrated oil company active in all spheres of the industry. Chevron UK Ltd handles all its North Sea Oil and gas

exploration and production ('upstream' operations) whilst refining and marketing ('downstream' operations) are carried out by Gulf Oil. In 1989 Gulf expanded its service station network with the purchase of the Telegraph group of sites and a year later it acquired Action Service Stations.

Approximately half the total number of sites selling Gulf products are company owned, the majority of all the retail outlets and other fuel customers being supplied by road tankers operated on behalf of Gulf by Tankfreight. Although, in rural locations some service stations accept deliveries from their nearest authorised Gulf distributor.

For many years Leyland was the favoured make of vehicle in Gulf's fleet, being supplemented more recently by models from Seddon Atkinson and Volvo.

FOOTNOTE
Chevron have now sold Gulf Oil (GB) to Shell UK. This sale including the service stations and Milford Haven refinery. Chevron have pulled out of petrol retailing to concentrate on oil and gas production. However, Gulf lubricants will still be available.

Above: Silvertown Lubricants Ltd was the precursor of Gulf Oil in the U.K. and was a leading supplier of lubricants in the early part of the century. This Hallford dates from about 1918 and is equipped for both bulk and canned deliveries. The Hallford marque did not survive the 1920s but its origins dated back to 1785. They made their first lorry in 1906.

Below: Silvertown Lubricants claimed to be pioneers of delivering lubricants in bulk to customers, often supplying storage tanks as well. This service continued when Gulf Oil took over. This Austin K4 was one such tanker operating in their fleet in the 1930s and 40s. Many of Gulf's customers were large operators such as bus companies - this photograph being taken at an Eastern National bus garage.

Left: This photograph dates from 1960/61 and is of an Albion Caledonian newly into service painted in Gulf's orange and blue livery of the period. The tanker is for bulk oil deliveries, although Gulf petrol was about to be another new brand on the market at the time. The Albion was a contract vehicle operated by Gilbraith Tankers of Accrington.

Main picture: Chevron became a retailing and distribution company in this country in 1968 when Texaco took complete control of Regent and disposed of approximately 100 service stations to Chevron. This chain expanded and large supply contracts were also won. By the late 1970s several terminals were in operation and this line-up of tankers was taken at Middlesbrough. The Leyland Bison and Buffalo were new in 1976 and, alongside, are two Atkinson Borderer tractor units and two AECs, one of which is a Mandator artic - the other is probably a Marshal six wheel rigid tanker.

Right: Chevron decided to use lightweight Volvo models and tanks fabricated from aluminium for maximum capacities and payloads. Even if the life of the tractor units was shorter than a heavier model the economics of such a policy still made sense over a period of time. This Volvo F7 artic entered service in 1981.

Gulf Oil (Chevron)

Above: Volvo F7 eight wheeler, new in 1982. It featured several weight saving components including aluminium wheels and lightweight "L'-ride suspension on the rear bogie. The aluminium tank was made by Crane Fruehauf and was designed to carry 5000 gallons of middle distillate. Just before the 1984 merger between Gulf and Chevron, Texaco bought Chevron's service stations which by then numbered almost 220.

Right: Much of Chevron's contract business was for middle distillates such as derv and gas oil, supplied to local authorities and county councils. This Volvo F86 drawbar outfit from the mid 1970s is an unusual type of tanker and such combinations have never been very common in oil company fleets. The Volvo and trailer could carry approximately 5300 gallons of derv or gas oil, depending upon the grade.

Left: In 1996 Gulf revitalised its brand image and a striking tanker livery of silver and blue was introduced. This Leyland Constructor six wheeler was new in that year and it has a five-compartment tank along with hose reel and metering equipment.

Below: Gulf Oil's distribution to service stations is handled by Tankfreight and this Volvo FL10 tractor unit and tri-axle semi-trailer is typical of their modern fleet. Tank capacity is 36,000 litres (7920 gallons) in six compartments. The location is West Bromwich terminal.

Left: In the mid 1990s Seddon Atkinson is owned by Iveco, although the Oldham-based firm is allowed a certain amount of autonomy. They use the Iveco group cab on most of their range and the Strato 210 is a popular model for distributors who require a good tank capacity on a compact four wheeler. With hose reel and metering equipment, S S Motors of Chatteris operate this 1994 version with a four-compartment tank of 13,000 litres capacity.

Mobil Oil Company Limited

The Mobil Oil Company Ltd is the oldest international oil company operating in Great Britain. It was founded in the USA in 1865 with the unusual name of Vacuum Oil. This name was derived from the residue of crude oil distillation under partial vacuum conditions which was found to possess excellent lubricating properties.

Charles Everest was a vice president of Vacuum Oil and he came to Liverpool in 1885 to establish the company's first overseas branch. Prior to then Vacuum Oil's products had been available in the UK with sales being handled by agents.

They sold a range of mineral oil based lubricants and greases, of which a steam cylinder oil was the first of its type to be marketed in this country. Previously lubricating oil and grease was blended from vegetable and animal fat bases and these decomposed to leave a gummy sediment on cylinder and bearing surfaces.

Charles Everest appointed one Charles Cheers Wakefield as his General Manager and after 14 years in this capacity with Vacuum Oil he left to found his own business which became famous for the 'Castrol' brand of lubricants.

For the first few years of trading Vacuum Oil's British subsidiary imported all of its supplies from the parent company. The various types of oil were transported across the North Atlantic in ships whose holds were full of wooden barrels.

Expansion was rapid and in 1893 Vacuum Oil transferred its head office from Liverpool to London. Three years later a warehouse was opened at Ferguson's Wharf, Millwall and this included facilities for oil blending and was the company's first overseas compounding plant.

As the 19th century drew to a close the business was prospering and branch offices and warehouses were opened at Cardiff, Liverpool, Newcastle, Glasgow and Manchester. By 1901 the growth had been such that a 'stand alone' British company, the Vacuum Oil Company Ltd, was established.

During 1903 a motor oil department was formed and the 'Mobiloil' trade name was used for the first time. The parent company had discovered that the word 'vacuum' could not be registered as a trade name in several countries where it operated. One year later its 'Gargoyle' trademark was registered and this rather strange feature adorned the drums and containers of Vacuum Oil's products for the next 40 years or so.

In the early period of this century the 'Mobiloil' name was extended to the complete range of products comprising lubricants for all purposes including harness oil and floor dressing.

Expansion was still rapid with a blending works being established at Birkenhead in 1905-6, followed by a similar facility at Wandsworth in 1913. This latter factory eventually replaced the original Millwall site. The outbreak of war in 1914 resulted in a huge demand for industrial oils in addition to the vast quantities of oils and greases supplied to the Armed Forces.

After the First World War the Vacuum Oil Company experienced several years of steady growth and consolidation and gained a reputation for premium quality lubricants. Many prestige contracts were won and much publicity was gained from the RMS Queen Mary in the 1930s when it held the Blue Riband for the fastest Atlantic crossing. This mighty liner's turbines and machinery were lubricated with Mobiloil.

When Britain found itself at war again in 1939 the Vacuum Oil Company, along with all the other similar firms became part of the Lubricating Oil Board. This government controlled organisation co-ordinated supplies and distribution to all branches of industry and transport.

The company suffered serious losses when its Birkenhead site was severely damaged as the result of enemy bombing in 1941. Production was increased at Wandsworth until the Merseyside factory was made workable again. After the trials and tribulations of the Second World War it was decided to replace the 'Gargoyle' trademark with the 'Pegasus' flying horse motif. This decision was taken in 1947 and the well known emblem is still a prominent feature today.

The decade of the 1950s was a significant one for the Vacuum Oil Company. Prior to then all its business in Great Britain was in lubricants. Stock oils for blending at Birkenhead and Wandsworth were shipped over from the USA but they had to be purchased in Dollars. Britain had a serious shortage of this currency but conversely, Middle Eastern crude oil could be bought in Pounds Sterling. Economically it therefore made sense to construct a

Left: This is Wandsworth blending plant shortly after it was built by Vacuum Oil in 1913. The site, although adjacent to the River Thames, was quite rural then and it had been the home and estate of the Watney brewing family. The vehicles in the photograph are a couple of GV electric carts operated by the Midland Railway, alongside horses and carts belonging to the Great Northern Railway.

refinery here and import crude oil for it to process.

Plans for a refinery at Coryton on the north bank of the Thames in Essex were drawn up, with the emphasis on its production being the refining of high grade lubricating stock oils. However, this would still have left about 85% of the output without an outlet through the Vacuum Oil Company. After a comprehensive research study of the market for other petroleum products a decision was made to enter the petrol and diesel market and some two years before the Coryton refinery opened in 1954, Mobilgas petrol was introduced.

With the refinery in production heating and steam raising fuel oils also became available and the well known firm of Charringtons handled the distribution and transportation of these products. In 1955 the company name was finally changed to the Mobil Oil Company Ltd.

With impetus provided by the expansion of the 1950s, Mobil consolidated its position and increased its market share for all its products during the 1960s. In 1964, in partnership with Regent and Total, Mobil formed an aircraft re-fuelling service at Heathrow. In the 1980s this became Mobil's Aviation Fuel Services. A few years after the initial Heathrow

Left: Wandsworth quickly expanded as demand for lubricants soared during World War One. In 1920 Vacuum Oil bought its first motor lorries, five AEC Y-type four tonners. More of the same were purchased in subsequent years and this line-up was photographed in the early 1920s. All are AECs apart from one, and note the massive stockpile of wooden oil barrels alongside.

As Vacuum Oil expanded in the first quarter of this century several depots were opened throughout the country. This is Glasgow depot in the 1920s, designed for access by lorries alongside its own railway sidings. The solid tyred lorry is an AEC Y-type.

Mobil Oil Company Limited

venture Mobil was able to set up Gatwick Re-fuelling Services at London's second airport. As Stansted airport expanded in the 1980s a similar operation was established there.

By 1968 the majority of Mobil's industrial lubricants customers were concentrated in the North and Midlands. This prompted the closure of their Wandsworth factory with the Birkenhead site being developed further to meet the demands of the clientele.

In the early 1960s Mobil commenced exploration under the North Sea and was rewarded when crude oil was discovered in October 1972. Their Beryl oil field came into production in mid 1976 providing a supply of crude oil for the Coryton refinery, which had been continuously modernised and up-rated since its construction in the 1950s.

Today Mobil is a fully integrated oil and petroleum company and its

activities encompass the whole process from exploration to retailing through its own service stations.

Since establishing a presence in Great Britain over 110 years ago, firstly as Vacuum Oil and then as Mobil, the company has operated its own transport fleet. Initially they used horses and carts. Then these were supplemented by steam wagons and then motor lorries. Through the years many makes of lorry have been used with AECs having had a presence for over 50 years until the demise of this marque in the 1970s.

Other makes operated have included Leyland, Thornycroft, Bedford, Austin, Morris, Scammell, ERF, Guy and Seddon Atkinson. Third party hauliers and contractors have been extensively hired and Charringtons in particular is a well-known name with a long association with Mobil and its precursor. Today the Mobil fleet of road tankers carrying

petrol and diesel fuel to service stations and other customers is predominantly ERF based and is operated in-house. It is supplemented with several national contractors to cope with fluctuating seasonal demands.

FOOTNOTE

As a result of the proposed joint venture between Mobil and BP announced as this book was in preparation (see footnote at the end of chapter 1), Mobil will eventually be returning to its roots in the UK and Europe by concentrating on lubricants. This agreement allows Mobil to hold 51% of the equity of the merged Mobil and BP lubricants businesses with BP retaining the remainder. Mobil will take operational control of the assets.

Left: Associated Daimler was a sales and marketing company established by AEC and Daimler in 1926. Each company continued to make commercial vehicles (and Daimler cars also) with a choice of AEC or Daimler engines. Most of the production under the Associated Daimler name were passenger chassis; goods vehicles were very rare. However, Vacuum Oil obviously operated some of these robustly constructed lorries. The Associated Daimler agreement was short-lived and was terminated in 1928.

Below: A superb photograph of a drawbar trailer outfit operated by Vacuum Oil in the 1920s. The livery conveys all the company information of name, Mobiloil brand name, Gargoyle trademark, etc. The lorry is an AEC, probably a Y-type converted to pneumatic tyres, with a four compartment tank. The trailer is a Dyson with twin compartment tank. The location is Vacuum's Birkenhead blending factory.

Left: Fleet number 4 was one of the first batch of AEC Y-types purchased in 1920. This photograph dates from 1923 and it is probable that the tank had only just been fitted as it appears to be new and freshly painted. The estimated capacity is 500 gallons.

Below: Scammell of Watford conceived its three wheeler tractor unit as a replacement for the horse and named the model 'Mechanical Horse'. There were two versions, a three tonner and a six tonner. Vacuum Oil operated this larger example of the model in 1935, seen here with a three compartment tank.

Above right: Two Bedfords for lubricants deliveries in service at Sunderland depot during the 1950s. Note the radiator blind on the O-type nearest the camera.

Right: The introduction of Mobilgas petrol in 1952 was a direct result of Vacuum's decision to construct a refinery at Coryton, Essex. However, until the refinery was commissioned in 1954, petrol was obtained from the other oil companies. This Bedford S-type artic was one of the new fleet of tankers purchased and is coupled to a 2400 gallon capacity tank semi-trailer.

Mobil Oil Company Limited

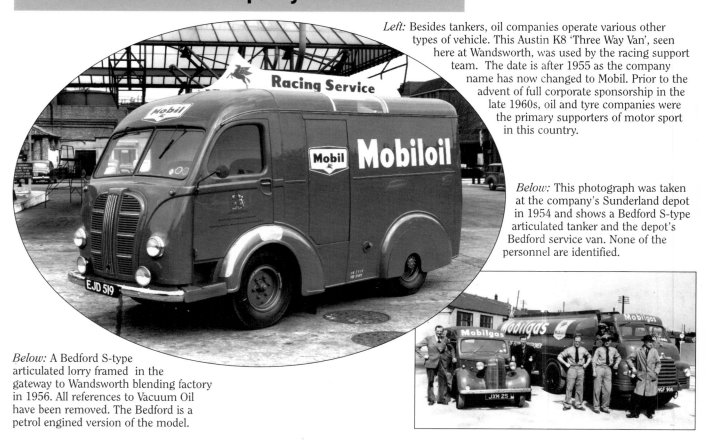

Left: Besides tankers, oil companies operate various other types of vehicle. This Austin K8 'Three Way Van', seen here at Wandsworth, was used by the racing support team. The date is after 1955 as the company name has now changed to Mobil. Prior to the advent of full corporate sponsorship in the late 1960s, oil and tyre companies were the primary supporters of motor sport in this country.

Below: This photograph was taken at the company's Sunderland depot in 1954 and shows a Bedford S-type articulated tanker and the depot's Bedford service van. None of the personnel are identified.

Below: A Bedford S-type articulated lorry framed in the gateway to Wandsworth blending factory in 1956. All references to Vacuum Oil have been removed. The Bedford is a petrol engined version of the model.

Left: The Leyland Comet model became a very popular medium weight vehicle in the 1950s with many examples of the type entering service with oil company fleets. This articulated version is coupled to a 2400 gallon capacity tank semi-trailer, the wintry location being Hanworth, Middlesex in the late 1950s.

Below: Bedford QL 4x4 refueller photographed in March 1958. It is equipped with a 950 gallon capacity tank made by the Steel Barrel Company of Uxbridge. Tankers such as these were used in a variety of locations where mobile refuelling was essential, such as civil engineering projects and airfields.

Left: The market for petrol grew rapidly during the 1950s and Mobil started to gain an increasing share of it. As their business expanded they added heavier and larger vehicles to their fleet. Two classic eight wheelers were caught on film on 17th June 1958 as they were about to depart for a night-time delivery: an AEC Mammoth Major Mk.III and Leyland Octopus 24.04.

Left: Mobil, as a leading lubricants specialist, provides many services to its customers. This is a transformer insulating oil service unit in action in the early 1960s at CEGB Tilbury Power Station. The equipment recycles the oil by cleaning and filtering it. It is based on an AEC Mammoth Major Mk.V six wheeler tractor unit and articulated semi-trailer.

Above: This is recorded as the first butane delivery to be made from Coryton to M Wiggins of Hereford in the early 1960s. The lorry is a Leyland Beaver artic with LPG tank semi-trailer. Note the fire extinguisher trolley in the foreground and numerous rail tank-cars in the background carrying Charrington's livery. This well known fuels distributor has handled the transport and distribution of Mobil fuel oils since the opening of Coryton refinery.

Right: When this photograph was taken in the early 1960s Mobil had been using AEC lorries for over 40 years. This Wandsworth based AEC Mandator Mk.V tractor unit with its four-in-line 4000 gallon capacity tank semi-trailer was photographed in an autumnal setting near Guildford.

Right: Mobil introduced ERF tractor units into their fleet in the 1960s. This Cummins powered ERF 6LV/L tractor unit was new in 1969 and it is seen coupled to a tandem axle semi-trailer with a seven compartment tank of 5700 gallon capacity. Towards the end of the decade Mobil replaced their red livery with a lighter grey and white design. The photograph dates from September 1972.

Left: ERF announced the new B-series range in 1974, these being their first models to have tilting cabs for easier engine access and maintenance. Mobil purchased several tractor units and these two 1975 examples were photographed at Coryton. Mobil had also increased their tank capacities to 6000 gallons (27,000 litres).

Left below: The 1972 increase in gross weights for eight and six wheelers (depending upon the wheelbase) resulted in rigid eights, in particular, becoming more popular as tankers for a time. This Seddon Atkinson example for 30 tons gvw operations, dates from 1977 and carries a seven compartment lubricating oils tank of 4620 gallon capacity.

Above: Seddon Atkinson became a new marque in Mobil's fleet in the mid 1970s and repeat orders were placed for several years. One of the 1980 intake, a 400 series tractor unit, is seen here and Mobil was also increasing its tank capacities by small amounts. The Seddon Atkinson has a seven compartment semi-trailer of 6400 gallon capacity.

Left: By the mid 1980s ERFs had virtually become the standard tractor units in Mobil's fleet. This C40 model, a rear steer six wheeler version, is coupled to a new tandem axle semi-trailer. The photograph was taken in 1987 and the tank is one of the recently introduced bottom loading types of six compartments and 35,000 litre capacity (7700 gallons).

The Shell Petroleum Company Limited

The formative years of Shell were different from those of many of the oil companies which have similarly become huge organisations. At the outset Shell was a petroleum transport and trading company. It did not explore for crude oil nor did it build refineries, although these activities became an integral part of its operations in due course.

The trading origins of the Samuel family which founded Shell can be traced to 1833 although it would be almost another 60 years before their oil industry involvement commenced. Marcus Samuel Snr opened a business in London's East End dealing in antiques, curios and oriental sea shells. The latter were so popular that regular shipments from the Far East were organised and soon a general importing and exporting business had been established.

Marcus Samuel died in 1870 and the firm came under the control of his two sons, Marcus Jnr and Samuel. In 1878 they formed two separate companies - Marcus Samuel & Company of London and Samuel Samuel & Company of Japan. Early in 1890 Marcus Samuel visited Batum on the Black Sea coast and was impressed by the scale of operations involved in exporting Russian produced oil. He foresaw a potentially large market for Russian kerosene or paraffin in the Far East if he could transport the product cheaply enough to undercut Standard Oil who had a monopoly of supply in the region.

To achieve the necessary economies the kerosene needed to be shipped in tankers through the Suez Canal. At that time the Canal owners had never allowed the passage of oil carrying ships. Undaunted, Marcus Samuel commissioned the construction of a tanker which satisfied the stringent safety regulations stipulated by the Suez Canal Company. In 1892 the first vessel laden with oil, SS Murex, passed through the Suez Canal on her maiden voyage from Batum to Singapore and Bangkok. Bulk storage facilities being built at several Far Eastern ports to ensure the long term supply of Russian kerosene.

By 1897 Samuel's petroleum business had grown to such an extent that he formed a separate company. This was named The 'Shell' Transport and Trading Company Ltd. This new enterprise continued to flourish and one year later began oil exploration and production. This resulted from Marcus Samuel obtaining an option on a concession in Dutch Borneo. A successful oil well was drilled and subsequently a refinery was opened at Balik Papan. The discovery of crude oil at Spindle Top, Texas, in 1901 provided the opportunity for Shell to handle its transportation and distribution. As a result of this initiative Shell Transport became the first oil company with world-wide sources of production and supplies of refined products. Standard Oil became so concerned about Shell's rate of expansion that it proposed a take-over but their approach was rebuffed by Marcus Samuel. However, it was not all plain sailing for Shell and problems were encountered in Borneo where the kerosene was of poor quality and the refinery problematic. Also certain contracts were not fulfilled in the Dutch East Indies.

A few years before Marcus Samuel commenced transporting kerosene, crude oil was discovered in Sumatra by a Dutch national. In 1890 he sought additional funding and converted his Provisional Sumatra Petroleum Company into the Royal Dutch Petroleum Company which was established in The Hague.

By the mid 1890s Royal Dutch was in strong competition with Shell and in order to compete more effectively started to construct tankers and storage facilities. They also set up a sales and marketing organisation. By 1903 Royal Dutch and Shell were competing in the same markets and also against Standard Oil. Their interests were becoming similar and after negotiations they agreed to form the Asiatic Petroleum Company with Rothschilds as the third partner. Asiatic Petroleum combined the distributing resources and sales organisations of Shell Transport and Royal Dutch in all Far Eastern markets and it also became the selling agent for East Indies oil and petroleum production throughout the world.

The period of the mid 1900s saw Royal Dutch benefiting from increased petrol sales whereas Shell's main strength was in fuel oil which was not in such great demand. Shell also started to suffer a decline in its supplies from Texas and replaced this source with kerosene from Romania. However, Standard Oil had large quantities of surplus kerosene which it dumped in

Above: Shell and Scammell pioneered the usage of articulated tankers in the early 1920s. Scammell designed these lorries complete - that is, the semi-trailers were an integral part of the combination and could not be easily disconnected. This was to be their practice for the next 45 years. Initially Scammell designed their 'six wheelers' for towing draw-bar trailers as well, but the concept was deemed illegal as, in effect, two trailers were being pulled. This was the second Scammell delivered in 1921.

Left: The early Scammell six wheelers did not have the characteristic large casting of the famous marque name on the radiator header tank. Fleet No.22 has received a covered cab and it is coupled to a semi-trailer for carrying petrol cans.

The Shell Petroleum Company Limited

Europe at very low prices which resulted in heavy losses for its competitors.

By 1907 competition in the oil industry was very fierce and Royal Dutch and Shell Transport agreed to merge their interests. Each company was to retain individual identities and this laid the foundations for the present day Royal Dutch/Shell Group. In 1907 two new operating companies were formed - a Dutch based exploration and production company and the Anglo-Saxon Petroleum Company for transportation and storage which had its head office in London. Royal Dutch and Shell respectively took 60% and 40% interests in each of these companies and this ratio of shareholding exists to this day in many hundreds of the Group operating companies world-wide. Returning once again to 1907 and the marketing of products remained the responsibility of the Asiatic Petroleum Company which was also based in London. In 1946 Asiatic changed its name to The Shell Petroleum Company Ltd.

Following the 1907 merger rapid expansion occurred and additional producing interests were acquired in several areas of the world. New refineries were constructed including Shell Haven located on the Essex bank of the River Thames. Shell entered the North American gasoline market with the purchase of a Californian based marketing company and by 1912 was producing oil in several states. By this same year the long expected growth for fuel oil was beginning and Shell received orders from the Royal Navy for boiler fuel, and by 1914 Shell petrol was becoming a well known brand in Great Britain and many other countries.

After the 1914-18 war expansion continued and by 1920 fuel oil bunkering stations for ships had been established at all major ports in the world. Shell widened its interests in the USA when the Shell Union Oil Corporation was formed in 1922 as a result of a merger of Shell's American interests and the Union Oil Company of Delaware.

In Great Britain Shell became the majority shareholder with 60% in Shell-Mex and B.P. in 1932. This was a partnership with Anglo-Persian for the marketing and retailing of both oil companies' fuel products.

Shell-Mex was a similar distributing organisation set up in 1919 when Shell had taken a financial interest in the Mexican Eagle Oil Company. Shell's assets in Mexico were nationalised in 1938. Shell-Mex and B.P. was to become one of the dominant forces in petrol retailing in Great Britain until the agreement was terminated in 1975.

In the 1930s, Shell also entered into several other joint marketing arrangements in many countries. Some measure of Shell's growth can be gauged from the crude oil production statistics for 1938 which show that this one company was responsible for 10% of the world's total.

In September 1939, at the outbreak of the Second World War, all Shell's British operations came under control of the emergency wartime Pool Petroleum Boards. By then Shell also had important chemicals interests which dated back to 1929. One of Shell Chemical Corporation's products, butadiene, was used for synthetic rubber production and it was made in large quantities to aid the war effort.

After the war Shell concentrated on replacing its damaged and lost assets. For example it lost 87 of its ocean going and coastal tankers as a result of enemy action. At the same time it started to meet new pressures on demand by providing extra production, refining and transport facilities. Exploration in new territories commenced and in this country Shell extended its refineries at Stanlow and Shell Haven.

By the mid 1950s output and sales were increasing dramatically both in the UK and overseas. In 1955 the business of the long-standing Anglo-Saxon Petroleum Company was vested in The Shell Petroleum Company which today is one of two Group holding companies for all Group interests outside of the United States.

The period of the late 1950s and early 1960s saw continuing annual increases in output and sales for Shell. During these years it supplied approximately 14% of the world's oil products.

Expansion in this country continued with new service stations being built and acquired and in 1963 Shell opened the first self-service site in England.

Exploration commenced in the North Sea in a joint venture with Esso and in 1966 Shell Expro, as the company was called, discovered the Leman gas reserves in the southern North Sea. In 1971 the massive Brent oil field was discovered by the same exploration company. Later in the 1970s further significant oil finds were made in other fields and Brent was recognised as the biggest discovery in the UK sector of the North Sea.

The dramatic price rise for crude oil resulting from the OPEC crisis of 1973, followed by a world-wide reduction in demand caused Shell to expand into other sources of energy. It started to ship liquefied natural gas in specially designed tankers to countries such as Japan which had no reserves of their own. Although oil, natural gas and chemicals remained the core activities for Shell, it began to develop interests in coal and metals during the decade of the Seventies.

With lessons learned from the traumas of the 1970s, Shell entered the 1980s with the aim of improving its efficiency through the rationalisation and automation of its distribution networks. The long-standing Shell-Mex and B.P. marketing arrangement was disbanded at the end of 1975 leaving Shell free to concentrate on building its own very strong brand image in petrol and diesel fuel retailing. Coupled with this, as the 1980s progressed, was a new range of high quality products and introduction of a variety of customer orientated services. These policies have continued into the 1990s.

The reduction in crude oil prices in the early 1990s resulted in Shell selling some of its more peripheral businesses and concentrating on its traditional core interests. Today not only is Shell one of the world's largest fully integrated oil companies, its substantial chemicals business added to its oil interests also places Shell as one of the

Left: By the time fleet no.75 entered service the more traditional Scammell styling had evolved although the chain drive and solid tyres were retained in the mid 1920s. Note the legend 'Scammell Six Wheeler' on the cab door. The semi-trailer is a frameless tank of five compartments.

Below: Three solid tyred Scammell six wheelers from the mid 1920s. These tankers are probably part of one of the convoys organised during the general strike of 1926. Note the large and elaborate 'Shell' logo on the rear of the tankers.

Left: Shell-Mex Ltd existed as a separate company from 1920 until 1932. It was a distribution organisation established when Shell had taken a financial interest in the Mexican Eagle Oil company. Shell-Mex built itself a substantial share of the fuel oil market. This Thornycroft from circa 1931 has rather a small tank for such a commodity, as most fuel oil customers were large consumers such as power stations and heavy industrial processes.

world's largest companies of any description.

Shell's road transport operations in the UK have involved very significant numbers of vehicles over the years. In the period before the formation of Shell-Mex and B.P. Shell operated several makes and it was one of the pioneers of articulated tanker usage with Scammell early in the 1920s. Scammell had a highly individualistic approach to lorry design and for many years their articulated tankers were conceived as complete units and tanks were very rarely separated from the tractor units.

The Shell and Scammell tradition continued from the 1920s through the Shell-Mex and B.P. years with the famous normal control Highwayman model and its forward control successor, the Handyman. Shell also operated a large fleet of Scammell's twin-steer Trunker tractor units and also considerable numbers of Scammell Routeman rigid eight wheelers.

Operating alongside the Scammells for many years were various AEC and Leyland lorries. After the demise of all these famous British makes Shell bought Volvos, Fodens and Seddon Atkinsons in the 1980s, with the last two marques still prominent in fleet of the mid 1990s.

Because of the sheer scale of Shell's operations it has always used contract hauliers to cope with seasonal fluctuations in demand. Some of its lubricants distribution is now contracted out and its own fleet of road tankers is so organised that deliveries to its filling stations and other fuel customers can be made on any day of the week.

Above right: Thornycroft Amazon, new in 1932 and apparently not quite complete as it is minus lights and mirrors. Whilst the tank has three filling hatches it appears to have only two outlet valves. The location is Smith Square, London SW1.

Right: AEC Monarch from 1931/2 for delivering petrol and lubricants in cans. This was the smallest lorry in the AEC range, designed to carry a payload of 5 tons. It has an early style of illuminated headboard. The West London Joint Railways parcels delivery van in the background is also of interest.

Top: Even though Shell had been one of the first oil companies to operate maximum capacity tankers in the early 1920s, in their Shell-Mex and B.P. period they also used some extremely small ones. This diminutive Albion had a 250 gallon capacity tank and was specially designed for delivering to sites with limited access such as mews locations in London.

Above: Some of the Scammell Mechanical Horse models did operate as rigids in addition to the thousands of artics used by the railway companies and others. This 1954 long wheelbase version carried a 450 gallon kerosene tank for local deliveries.

Left: An ex W.D. Bedford 'OY' with Thompson 'Essex' 800 gallon refueller built when new vehicles were in short supply, post-war production being directed at the export market. It featured a single compartment tank and was capable of loading fuel at a rate of 60 g.p.m.

The Shell Petroleum Company Limited

Below: Dennis Jubilant articulated tanker operated by Shell-Mex and B.P. It was new in the mid 1950s and is coupled to a four compartment tank semi-trailer of 2500 gallons capacity.

Right: Changes in legislation in the mid 1960s forced Scammell to abandon its long-held belief in normal control (bonneted) articulated lorries. Even so their Trunker rear-steer six wheeler forward control model displayed many of Scammell's individualistic ideas and designs. Even the seven compartment tank is unusual with its bogie's rearmost axle located beyond the end of the tank.

Left: Yes, this is MLC753, the AEC Mammoth Major Mk.III eight wheeler seen on pages 12/13 in Chapter One. The nearside was sign-written for 'Shell', the offside for 'B.P.'. This was common practice in the period of the Shell-Mex and B.P. agreement.

Below: Fulham Terminal of Shell-Mex and B.P. in the early 1960s as viewed over the top of an AEC Mandator Mk.V articulated tanker. Other prominent lorries include an AEC Mercury, Bedfords (S-type and TK), Albion (National), Leyland Comet and Dodge (White Spirit).

Above: Scammell Trunker Mk.2 in the Shell livery of the early 1970s. This scheme is virtually the basis of the modern Shell livery with the continuous red band just partly discarded.

Right: The separate companies of Seddon and Atkinson had supplied vehicles to Shell-Mex and B.P. The merged combine of Seddon Atkinson had great success with its 400 series tractor units in the mid 1970s. Shell was a purchaser of the model and this example entered service in 1977.

Right: Volvo F7 twin steer units joined the Shell fleet in the late 1970s, they being specifically designed as replacements for the fleet of Scammell Trunkers then working with the LPG semi-trailer tanks. Any consideration as to converting those tanks to a two-axle configuration being ruled out due to the complications involved in the management of stress as a consequence of undertaking welding work on a pressurised vessel.

Left: There was still a requirement for rigid eight wheeled tankers in the early 1980s. By then Leyland's offering was based on a chassis designed by Scammell and named Constructor. This Rolls Royce powered version is unusually running on super-single rear tyres.

Left: A rare make in the Shell fleet in 1982 was this Mercedes 1628 articulated aircraft refueller. This is a conventional design for such vehicles and is registered for public roads usage as well as airport duties.

Below: In 1992 Shell introduced tri-axle semi-trailers into their fleet. Based on Fruehauf running gear they are able to carry 400 litres more than a tandem axle design because the combined unladen weight of the tractor unit and trailer is reduced. A Seddon Atkinson Strato provides the motive power.

Shell-Mex and B.P.

Before the merger of Shell and Anglo-Persian's marketing interests in 1932 each of the constituent companies had pursued its own retailing policy. Shell-Mex was itself a joint venture between Shell and the Mexican Eagle Oil Company and much of its business was located in heavy fuel oils.

Shell was a reasonably strong petrol brand in 1932. Since the early years of the century Anglo-Persian had entered into several joint ventures with Shell, either through Shell Transport and Trading and/or with Royal Dutch/Shell and their subsidiary companies. These trading and marketing agreements were in place in many countries in addition to Great Britain.

In the first half of the century Anglo-Persian and its successor was primarily an exploration and production company. Even though it was a major oil producer it had secured outlets for its production through trading agreements with other oil companies and by securing massive long term supply contracts such as the one with the Royal Navy.

It was not until 1917 that Anglo-Persian started to build its own distribution and retailing network for petrol and light distillates when it took control of the British Petroleum

Company Ltd and its 'B.P.' brand name.

When Shell-Mex and B.P. was formed by these two major companies it resulted in a marketing and distribution organisation which dominated British fuel retailing. Shell held 60% of the equity and Anglo-Persian held 40%. The road tanker fleet operated by Shell-Mex and B.P. was huge and comprised most British built makes and models in varying numbers.

The heavy vehicles were predominantly supplied by Scammell, Leyland and AEC. In the medium weight category of smaller capacity tankers Leyland Comets, AEC Mercurys and various models from Albion, Foden, Dennis, Thornycroft and Seddon featured. The lighter tankers included models from Bedford, Austin and Morris.

Several colour schemes and liveries were used during the 43 years of the partnership - the rich green and red of the 1950s and the yellow and white of the 1960s are probably the best remembered ones. It was usual for the tanks to be signwritten 'Shell' on one side and 'B.P.' on the other.

During the course of Shell-Mex and B.P. the long established brands of National Benzole and Power Petroleum came under its control.

Both these names of petrol continued to be marketed and sold and tankers were liveried appropriately for them.

Eventually the partners in the venture decided they wanted autonomy in their affairs. At the end of 1975 the Shell-Mex and B.P. agreement was terminated to allow each company to pursue its own marketing and retailing policy.

BP briefly re-introduced the National Benzole brand in the early 1980s when the oil industry and its trading agreements were placed under scrutiny by the Monopolies Commission.

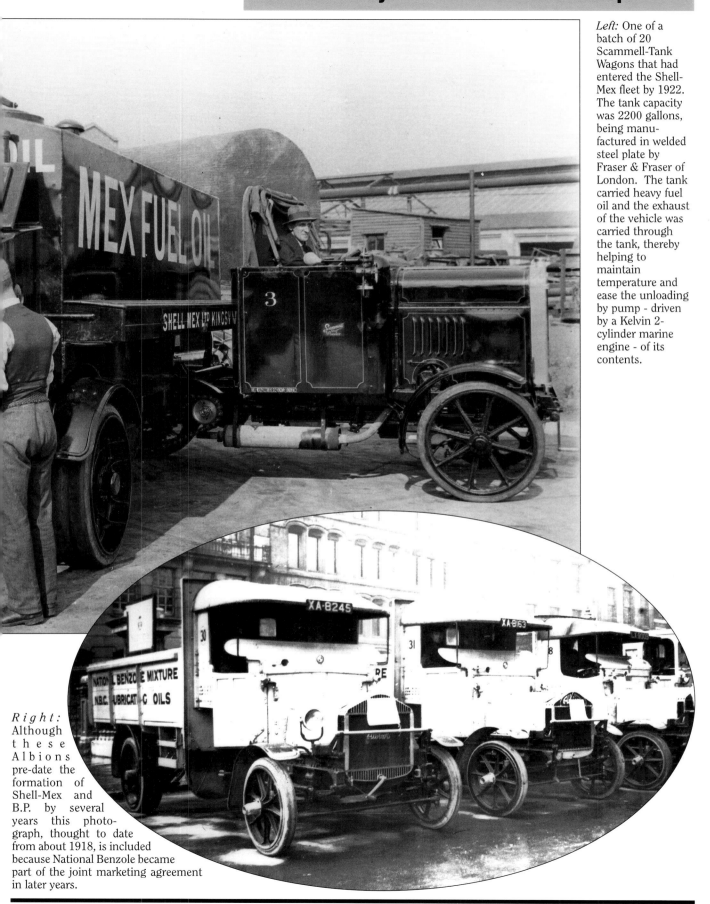

Left: One of a batch of 20 Scammell-Tank Wagons that had entered the Shell-Mex fleet by 1922. The tank capacity was 2200 gallons, being manufactured in welded steel plate by Fraser & Fraser of London. The tank carried heavy fuel oil and the exhaust of the vehicle was carried through the tank, thereby helping to maintain temperature and ease the unloading by pump - driven by a Kelvin 2-cylinder marine engine - of its contents.

Right: Although these Albions pre-date the formation of Shell-Mex and B.P. by several years this photograph, thought to date from about 1918, is included because National Benzole became part of the joint marketing agreement in later years.

Shell-Mex and B.P.

Above: National Benzole Thornycroft from the late 1920s. It has a twin compartment tank of an estimated 500 gallons capacity. National was one of the largest petrol distributors during the 1920s with a strong brand name and image.

Above right: Scammell conceived and perfected its frameless tanker design and hundreds of the various models served Shell-Mex and B.P. over the years. This example is typical of the design of the late 1930s and 1940s, it having single balloon tyres on the main load bearing axles.

Right: An early post-war Shell BP 'Devon' fuelling pumping unit by Thompson Bros. based on a Fordson 7V chassis. Note the Leyland Comet tankers in the background awaiting painting and lining out.

Left: With the formation of Shell-Mex and B.P. in 1932 the combined road transport fleet became huge. Scammells had been bought in quantity by Shell in the 1920s and this famous marque was to have a prominent place in the new organisation for the whole of its existence. This Scammell six wheeler, a petrol engined model, is seen in the new livery of 1932.

Right: A 1954 Dennis Centaur which was converted to 'Chinese Six' format by adding a second steering axle. This enabled it to have an increased capacity tank, 2400 gallons, as opposed to the standard 1500 or 2000 sizes on two axle vehicles of the period.

Right: The Leyland Beaver model was a premium quality product and really too heavy to make a suitable four wheeled tanker. Complete with its four compartment Steel Barrel Co tank, the vehicle has an unladen weight of over 6 tons, limiting its legal payload in the 1950s to less than 2000 gallons.

Below: In the mid 1950s the rigid eight wheeler was flagship in any road transport fleet. Shell-Mex and B.P. operated hundreds of such vehicles as tankers and AEC Mammoth Major Eight Mk.IIIs were one of the most popular type. This six compartment tank of 4000 gallons capacity, and indeed the complete vehicle, has a superb livery. The distinctive sliding door cab is by Reeve and Kenning. The Dennis alongside - by way of contrast to what was then the largest capacity tankers operated by Shell-Mex and B.P. - has a diminutive tank of 500 gallons capacity.

Shell-Mex and B.P.

Left: During the 1950s several of the tank manufacturers fabricated prototypes from aluminium as a means of reducing weight. This is one such tank on a Dennis 50 cwt chassis. The completed tanker had an unladen weight of 2 tons 8 cwt thereby allowing it to carry a similar weight payload of 600 gallons.

Right: A Leyland Hippo-based Thompson 'Stafford' aircraft refueller, examples of which entered service with the company in the mid 1950s. As aircraft payload and size increased, so indeed did the vehicles required to refuel them. The tank had a capacity of 8,500 gallons. Note the absence of any registration number - these impressive articulated vehicles being designed for working within the confines of the country's international airports.

Right: Aircraft refuellers have always had characteristics far different from those of road-going tankers. This Leyland Steer 'Chinese Six' with a large crew cab was new to Shell-Mex and B.P. in the early 1950s.

Below: An example of the Thompson 'Cornwall' aircraft refueller from the same period. The tank on the Leyland Hippo has a capacity of 3,300 gallons, whilst the drawbar trailer tank carried 4,500 gallons. The location appears to be the rather primitive international facilities of London's Heathrow, then situated on the airport's northern perimeter. This vehicle would have been used to fuel aircraft like the piston-engined Boeing Stratocruiser, then the leading long haul airliner, in service with PanAm and B.O.A.C. (British Overseas Airways Corporation).

Right: This 1957 Albion Caledonian eight wheeler was in pristine condition for the Commercial Motor Show, held at Earls Court. Albion was part of Leyland Motors and whilst the Caledonian had a Leyland cab and engine its chassis, gearbox and axles were Albion components.

Right below: The AEC Mercury became a popular basis for four wheel tankers in the late 1950s. A quality vehicle, it was exactly one ton lighter unladen than the Leyland Beaver shown on page 77, giving increased tank capacity and payload.

Below: National Benzole was still marketed strongly within the Shell-Mex and B.P. arrangements in the 1950s and 1960s. This BMC Morris 7-tonner was destined for the 1958 Commercial Motor Show. It has a four compartment tank with fairings which were quite common on many National tankers.

Left: Rather surprisingly, AEC did not offer a medium weight Mercury derived six wheeler until 1960. There was a demand for such a model and many operators had third axles fitted by specialist firms such as York, Boys and Primrose. This is one such late 1950s conversion on a Mercury Mk.I vacuum assisted hydraulic braked model.

Below: The basic design and style of Scammell's articulated eight wheeler remained unchanged for over 30 years. Engineering improvements and innovations were incorporated over the years and the model became known as the Highwayman from the 1950s. Balloon tyres are still retained in this photograph and the rear bogie has Scammell's own design of rubber suspension.

Below: This 'Yorkshire' aircraft refueller had just been delivered from the Bradley Engineering Works of Thompson Brothers when photographed in 1960. The light alloy tank had a capacity of 10,000 gallons with the necessary motive power being provided by the appropriately named AEC Mk.V Mammoth Major. Such large vehicles are now mainly a product of the past - fuel now being pumped underground direct from an airport's tank farm on its perimeter to the aircraft ramp and loaded via a mobile hydrant dispenser unit.

Above: The Mammoth Major Mk.V introduced by AEC in 1958 was a completely re-designed model. The chassis height had been lowered and this coupled with a new suspension gave it improved stability when carrying tanker bodywork. Consequently the AEC Mk.V eight wheeler became a firm favourite with several oil companies and Shell-Mex and B.P. placed many of them in service. This example has a 4000 gallon capacity tank.

Left: Scammell built this prototype Trunker in 1963. It was an unconventional design and had a horizontally mounted Gardner 6HLX '150' engine in mid chassis. The gearbox was under the cab. The tank semi-trailer was a frameless design of 3750 gallons capacity. Shell-Mex and B.P. had a long history of testing prototype lorries; several photographs exist of lorries with air suspension, disc brakes and other examples of experimentation long before such components became commonplace on large commercial vehicles.

Left: 1964 Leyland Octopus 'Power Plus'. This model was introduced in 1961 to replace the Octopus 24.04 eight wheeler. The LAD cab, seen in this photograph, was not really suitable for fitting to a premium quality chassis, it providing cramped conditions and a noisy environment for the driver. This example also has the lighter Albion rear bogie which was a weight saving option.

Above: This ERF tanker, photographed when new in November 1962 outside the Palace of Westminster, was powered by a 6.5 litre Rolls Royce 88R petrol engine. The vehicle's attributes being seen as an advantage when making fuel oil deliveries to environmentally sensitive locations demanding quieter running characteristics, such as hospitals. The capacity of the Alfred Miles welded alloy tank was 4000 gallons.

Right: The Construction and Use Regulations changes in 1964 signalled the end for Scammell's Highwayman model and they replaced it with a conventional design of articulated tractor unit. This Scammell Trunker Mk.2 was new in 1965 and its rear steer six wheeled design enabled it to operate at the newly introduced maximum gcw of 32 tons.

Right: The Scammell Highwayman and their fuel oil semi-trailers were replaced by examples of the marque's Handyman two-axle tractor unit coupled to new 4600 gallon tanks. The Handyman combination pumped its heavy fuel load off, this being a new innovation as a high percentage of the Highwayman fleet off-loaded their fuel oil tanks by the use of air pressure. The Mk.2 version illustrated was new to the company in 1965 being fitted with Leyland's Power Plus 680. The Rolls Royce Eagle unit was offered as an option.

Above: Even though there was a massive switch to articulated vehicles in the mid 1960s, because of the increased payloads they offered over traditional rigid eights, examples of the latter types continued to be bought. This Guy Big J entered service in 1967.

Left: An AEC Mercury with single compartment tank dedicated to delivering electrical oils for transformers and sub stations. The vehicle entered service with the company in 1972, the legend on the cab door carries the names of Shell-Mex and B.P., National Benzole and Power.

Texaco Limited

Texaco Ltd has had a presence in Great Britain for many years. The company has been involved in the oil and petroleum market here under several names because of partner-ships and joint ventures.

These arrangements are quite common and often come about because one particular partner might have surplus quantities of product which can compensate for the other partner's shortages. They can also agree to joint marketing ventures as a means of spreading the risks involved in entering a particular market.

The Texaco Petroleum Products Company was established in Britain in 1916 and this was one of the roots of the present day company, the other being Trinidad Leaseholds which was formed in 1913.

An oil find in the USA resulted in the formation of the Texas Fuel Company in 1901 and in the following year the name was shortened to the Texas Company. Even though 'Texaco' was adapted as the cable address it was to be many years before this title came to prominence. In its early years the Texas Company was an exploration undertaking, selling crude oil for refining and processing, however by 1905 it had built its own refinery and

opened a European subsidiary.

In 1916 the Texaco Petroleum Products Company was formed in Great Britain it being a subsidiary of the American parent company. At this stage petrol was a minority interest, the majority of the business being in lubricating oils, asphalt and wax. In 1928 the London head office relocated from The Strand to Millbank and this coincided with a change of name to the Texas Oil Company. It was not until 1959 that the parent company adopted the familiar Texaco name.

The Central Mining and Investment Corporation, an owner of South African gold mines, formed Trinidad Leaseholds in 1913. It purchased an oil lease for 81 square miles of land in Trinidad from the British Government. After problems initially, by 1917 Leaseholds had discovered enough crude oil to justify building a refinery on Trinidad. A decision which was to have vital significance for Britain in future years.

By 1930 Leaseholds was refining high octane petrol and aviation spirit which was sold through outlets in North America and the West Indies. It sought a distributor in the United Kingdom and purchased the business of Burt, Boulton and Haywood. The

latter company was a petroleum wholesaler whose trademark was 'Regent' and their storage depot was at Prince Regent Wharf on the Isle of Dogs.

Burt, Boulton and Haywood was quite a small firm with just sixteen staff and four road tankers. However, they expanded very rapidly by obtaining supply contracts with large bus companies. Once such a contract had been secured a depot or terminal would be opened nearby to obtain further business in that locality. In the 1930s individual service stations sold several brands of petrol and competition was fierce. This made it difficult for Regent to obtain a presence on forecourts, so they adopted a new approach and persuaded many garage owners to retail Regent exclusively. This was the start of solus trading, so familiar today.

When war was declared in 1939 the Petroleum and Lubricating Oil Boards were formed to control the production and distribution of all such products. All the oil companies pooled their resources under the direction of the Government. Leasehold's Trinidad refinery played a vital role between 1939-45. Because it was remote from the enemy, it was able to supply high octane aviation spirit and it is reputed that the Spitfires and Hurricanes of the Battle of Britain were fuelled exclusively from Leasehold's Trinidad refinery.

Even though peace returned in 1945 supplies were still rationed and the pooling arrangements continued for several more years. The Texas Oil Company remained strong in the lubricants market but was relatively weak in petrol retailing. Its parent company had access to Middle Eastern supplies of diesel and gas oil. Leaseholds with its Regent brand had a strong diesel fuel and petrol distribution network.

In 1947 Leaseholds and the Texas Oil Company agreed to market the full ranges of both companies' products under the Regent Oil Company throughout the United

A Century of Petroleum Transport

Left: A Leyland Beaver from the mid 1930s and put into service just a few years after Trinidad Leaseholds had acquired Burt, Boulton and Haywood together with their Regent brand. It has a four compartment tank made by Butterfields of Shipley.

Below: This photograph was taken on 13th September 1954 when the Regent Oil Company was jointly owned by Trinidad Leaseholds and Caltex. The Bedford S type or 'Big Bedford' model was launched in the early 1950s, many were petrol engined, as is this example. It is fitted with a four compartment tank. Note how closely positioned are the petrol pumps.

Kingdom. This arrangement had only been in force for a few weeks when Caltex bought the (American) Texas Oil Company's British business. This resulted in Regent being owned equally by Leaseholds and Caltex.

Caltex itself had been formed in 1936 as a joint venture between the Texas Oil Company and Standard Oil Company of California.

In Summer 1948 the Petroleum and Lubricating Oil Boards were disbanded although 'Pool' petrol was sold until 1952. Later in 1948, Regent bought the British interests and distribution facilities of Russian Oil Products Ltd.

During the 1950s Regent persuaded many more dealers to agree to solus trading and the company started to acquire its own service station sites. It also began to gain a reputation for the high quality of its products. In 1956 Leaseholds changed its name to the Trinidad Oil Company.

By the mid 1950s Regent was in dire need of a British based refinery to process Middle Eastern crude oil which was a third of the price of Trinidadian crude. Regent's profits were not sufficient to fund the cost of a new refinery and the Trinidad Oil Company could no longer afford to be an equal partner with Caltex in Regent. To resolve these difficulties the (American) Texas Oil Company bought the Trinidad Oil Company and also 75% of Regent. Caltex retained a 25% share of that business.

During the 1960s Regent embarked on a decade of very high capital expenditure. In 1964 a new refinery was opened at Pembroke and exploration in the North Sea started. Also in 1964 Regent, along with Mobil and Total, established an aircraft refuelling service at Heathrow,

This was also a period of intense competition in petrol retailing and Regent's market position weakened. During 1967 Caltex (Europe) was split up so Texaco, as the company had become in 1959, took full ownership of Regent. The Regent name and trademark was

discontinued with the Texaco logo replacing it. About one hundred service stations were rebranded as Chevron but the remainder, some three hundred in total, were changed to Texaco. The first one to re-open under the new scheme was in Northern Ireland.

To increase its share of the market Texaco came to an arrangement with Heron Service Stations. Initially it was to supply petrol for five years and then acquire certain of their sites. This was similar to an agreement dating back to the Regent years and the Blue Star Group. In 1972 Stations Supreme was formed from Blue Star and Heron sites and this was wholly owned and operated by Texaco.

After ten years of exploration Texaco was the first oil company to sell petrol from North Sea oil in 1975. In 1983 the company bought Chevron's European assets and this deal included a further 219 service stations. It will be recalled that 100 of these had been part of the original Regent chain.

During all these years of commercial activity Texaco has continued to invest in the Pembroke refinery by constantly updating it and increasing its output. Today, Texaco is one of Britain's largest fully integrated oil companies being involved in all aspects of the exploration, production and retailing chain.

In the early years of Leaseholds and Regent several makes of vehicles were used, although AEC was the favoured marque. This continued after the 1939-45 war and when the Regent marketing campaign started in earnest in the late 1940s, the road tanker fleet consisted mainly of former Pool Petroleum tankers. These were Maudslay Mogul four wheelers and Atkinson six and eight wheelers. All were powered by AEC engines.

During the 1950s AEC Monarchs, Mammoth Majors and Mercurys were prominent along with several Atkinsons and Guys. With the switch to a predominantly articulated tanker fleet in the mid 1960s, Regent and

Texaco relied almost exclusively on the AEC Mandator tractor unit with AEC Mercurys providing the bulk of the rigid fleet. In total they operated several hundred AECs of all types.

With the demise of the AEC marque in 1977 Texaco continued to buy Leyland Marathons in quantity. These were also built at Southall and when the factory closed in 1979 production of this model continued at Scammell, Watford. When the Leyland T45 Roadtrain replaced the Marathon, Texaco became a large operator.

The depressed years of the early 1980s caused Texaco to examine all of its operations and a policy decision was taken in 1985 to contract out all of its road tanker deliveries. This resulted in, firstly, TankFreight winning this very large contract and then Wincanton took over all the company's deliveries to service stations and commercial customers.

Right: Delivering drums of lubricants the old fashioned way without the benefit of any handling aids such as a tail-lift. This Fordson Thames 'Costcutter', entered the Regent fleet in the early 1950s.

Above: A Bedford S type articulated tanker from the mid 1950s. At the time Bedford did not manufacture their own diesel engine so diesel powered versions, such as this, were fitted with the troublesome Perkins R6 unit. The vehicle is fitted with a four compartment tank. Note the Royal warrant.

Above: The Regent fleet of the 1950s contained the products of number of British manufacturers, this Albion being typical of the smaller tankers employed. It has a three compartment tank of 1500 gallons capacity.

Above: Regent changed its livery in the early 1960s to a much simpler red design, this Guy Invincible eight wheeler entering service carrying the new paint scheme. The model's cab styling was considered very advanced and futuristic for the time.

Right: There is no date for this photograph but it could be winter 1960 when the Fina depot at Stourport on Severn was flooded and Regent also had a terminal there, which is clearly identifiable in the background. The AEC Mammoth Major Mk.III eight wheeler makes an impressive bow wave as it exits the gate.

Left: Some idea of Regent's diverse vehicle buying policy can be gauged by these two tankers. An Atkinson Mk.II eight wheeler - very much a premium quality product - and a Bedford TK, a mass produced example from the cheaper end of the market. The Bedford TK range was introduced in 1960 and this photograph dates from that period.

Above: Texaco became the sole owner of Regent in 1967 and the first conversions to the new brand took place in Northern Ireland in 1967. The Regent livery was retained - just the name was changed and this Bedford TK artic, Leyland Octopus and Bedford van were all displaying the Texaco logo at Carrickfergus.

Above left: This AEC Mammoth Major Mk.V eight wheeler was put into service in December 1962. It was photographed in the calibration bay at Stourport on Severn. It has a seven compartment tank of 4000 gallons capacity. These were some of the most stylish and attractive tankers of the period.

Left: This photograph depicts the Regent livery of the 1960s and features an Atkinson Mk.II eight wheeler tanker with 3600 gallon tank. The location is the Market Square, Wells, Somerset - the Cathedral providing an impressive backdrop.

All the major oil companies have a record of innovation and this photograph is notable on two counts. The Atkinson tractor unit is fitted with a 5-speed semi automatic gearbox (Self Changing Gears), mated to a Cummins 220 engine and the tank was the first filament wound glassfibre type. It was a single compartment tank, 5000 gallons capacity, for fuel oil. Registered in 1967 this was one of the last new vehicles to carry the Regent livery.

Texaco Limited

Left: Regent and Texaco operated a number of converted four wheelers. Primrose Engineering added a rear steer axle to provide increased payloads where access for an eight wheeler or articulated lorry was difficult. This Guy Warrior registered in 1967 was one of several Guys and the other conversions were based on AEC Mercury chassis. These six wheelers operated mainly in London.

Left below: By the mid 1960s, Regent was rationalising its tanker fleet into three makes of chassis - AEC, Atkinson and Guy. This Guy Big J tractor unit (the 'Big J' designated Guy's ownership by Jaguar Cars) was one of the new 30 tons gross train weight lorries evaluated in 1966. It is coupled to a YEWCO (Yorkshire Engineering & Welding Company) tank semi-trailer of 5500 gallons capacity and seven compartments.

Right and below: After deciding on three core marques in the mid 1960s for tanker duties, Texaco rationalised even further towards the end of the decade with AEC becoming the favoured make. Compared with the situation only a few years previously, the tanker fleet became virtually a two model operation; a smallish number of AEC Mercury four wheelers and a large quantity of AEC Mandator artics. This Mercury has a four compartment tank with hose reel equipment and the Mandator is coupled to a YEWCO 6000 gallons seven compartment tank semi-trailer.

Below: During the mid 1970s Texaco introduced Leyland Lynx tractor units for smaller articulated tanker duties. The Lynx was a more powerful alternative to an AEC Mercury tractor unit for medium weight operations but its complex '500 series' fixed cylinder head engine caused the Leylands to be far less reliable than the AECs. This Leyland Lynx is coupled to a single axle semi-trailer of 4000 gallons capacity.

Below: This 1972 Ford D series used for lubricants deliveries had a tank for bulk oil orders and a tail-lift for easy unloading of drums.

Texaco Limited

Left: After the demise of the AEC marque in 1977 Texaco switched to the Leyland Marathon model as the replacement for the AEC Mandator. The Marathon was designed by AEC and launched in 1973. It continued to be built at Southall until the factory was closed in 1979. Texaco became one of the largest users of the Marathon and the first large order they placed specified the naturally aspirated L12 engine in place of the standard turbo-charged unit. In both cases the engine was a direct development of the AEC AV760 engine.

Below: In 1985 Texaco decided to contract out their distribution and deliveries to Tankfreight. The livery was changed and whilst the contractor took over Texaco's fleet of tankers, such as the remaining Leyland Marathons and newer Roadtrains, new models were introduced such as the Scania 92M seen in this photograph.

Right: Scania 92M from 1986, coupled to a six compartment tank semi-trailer, undertaking a delivery to a Texaco service station. Note the petrol prices of the mid 1980s.

Below: Volvo equipment was introduced by Tankfreight in 1986. This smart FL10 tractor unit is pictured coupled to a six compartment tank semi-trailer.

Right: The late 1980s saw a completely changed livery for Texaco, replacing one which had originated almost 30 years previously in the era of Regent. Leyland Roadtrains were still in service and being purchased by Tankfreight. This is a rear steer six wheeled tractor unit coupled to a tandem axle semi-trailer.

Total Oil Great Britain Ltd

Total Oil Products (GB) Ltd entered the UK market in 1955, it being a wholly owned subsidiary of Total SA which was founded in France in 1924.

The arrival of Total in Great Britain was met with plenty of interest by the established oil and petroleum companies. It was the first time for over a decade that a new oil company had sought to enter the marketplace here. For the first two years Total's business was handled by agents but in 1957 it started to recruit its own staff to promote the brand.

By 1959 Total had built up a marketing area in London and the Home Counties and all the products were shipped from France to London and Coastal's terminal at Canvey Island. From there a modest fleet of road tankers, each of 1500 gallons capacity, transported fuel to mainly commercial customers. These included users such as bus companies, haulage contractors and local authority transport depots.

In the late 1950s many homes and businesses still relied upon paraffin for heating purposes and it was a buoyant market dominated by well known brands such as Esso Blue and Aladdin Pink. Total introduced Riviera Golden paraffin and it started to gain a significant share of the sales. It also made domestic consumers aware of the Total name.

In 1960 the company opened its first service station at Bushey in Hertfordshire and within a short period the Total brand of petrol was becoming well known. Its acceptance amongst motorists was accelerated by the introduction of trading stamps, a sales gimmick which revolutionised the petrol retailing business. At that time in the early 1960s, unlike today, many cars were owned and used purely for pleasure by private motorists. Petrol was usually bought either by brand or at a garage local to the car driver's home. In effect, the giving of trading stamps reduced the retail price of petrol so drivers started to seek out service stations offering stamps. These were later exchanged for gifts and merchandise when sufficient had been accumulated.

During the 1960s Total expanded rapidly and a network of depots and terminals was opened throughout the country. In 1967 the name was changed to the present one of Total Oil Great Britain Ltd. The following year was notable for the opening of Lindsey Oil Refinery on Humberside, this facility being jointly owned with Fina plc.

In 1970 Petropolis was formed to operate certain Total owned service stations and during that decade oil exploration commenced in the North Sea.

After becoming well established in the fuel market Total acquired a lubricating oil blending and grease manufacturing plant at Ferrybridge, West Yorkshire. This provided the company with the means to offer a comprehensive portfolio of products and the ability to serve all types of customers from motorists to industrial concerns, power stations and airlines.

Acquisitions in the 1990s have included businesses specialising in industrial bitumens, LPG bottling and distribution and general aviation services.

In the early years of operations in Great Britain, Total used several makes of vehicle including Dodge, AEC, Albion and Ford. AEC soon became the prominent marque in the road tanker fleet. After the demise of that famous make in the mid 1970s, DAF became the usual choice.

Total Oil Great Britain Ltd is now a fully integrated oil and petroleum company active in all aspects of the business. It still operates its own fleet of road tankers for fuel deliveries to service stations and other commercial customers and, in addition to DAFs, some ERFs and Ivecos are now in service. Other products such as bitumen, white spirit and LPG are transported by third party contractors.

Right above: The first tanker in the United Kingdom to be painted in the Total livery. The photograph was taken in 1959, coinciding with Total's announcement of its marketing plans for the introduction of the brand that was new to this country. The LAD cabbed Dodge is making its way around the statue of Eros in Piccadilly Circus, London.

Right: This was the rather bleak scene at Holehaven Terminal, Canvey Island in autumn 1960. It is a good example of top loading procedures in the days before loading racks were covered. Two AEC Mercurys and a Dodge are in view and the personnel identified are Ted Windsor (looking up), Charles Windsor (white overalls), Joe Swanson and Jimmy Francis (hands in pockets).

Above: This rear view of several Total tankers was taken at an unknown location in the early 1960s but it highlights the relatively simple but very effective Total livery. SHJ275 is an Albion, SXV605 is either a Dodge or Ford and the third tanker is plainly an AEC Mercury. Most of the tank capacities were 1500 gallons.

Above: Leeds Terminal fleet line-up in 1973 and on view are two AEC Mercurys, four AEC Mammoth Major eight wheelers, two AEC Mandator articulated outfits and two Volvo F86 artics. Volvo was still a relatively new make in this country then but had already established a good reputation for the quality and comfort of their lorries.

Left and right: The location is the loading rack at Leeds and four AECs - three Mammoth Majors and a Mercury - together with a Volvo F86 artic are ready to leave the terminal. The AEC Mammoth Major eight wheelers carried four compartment tanks of 4000 gallons capacity. Even though this was in 1973 and four axle articulated vehicles could legally operate at 32 tons gcw, four axle rigids such as these were restricted to 26 tons gvw. However, within a few months of this photograph being taken, changes in legislation would allow some eight wheelers to run at 30 tons gvw.

Total Oil Great Britain Ltd

Right: The AEC Mercury is not registered but the price of oil and the prices on the petrol and derv pumps in 'old money' date this photograph as pre-decimalisation, and probably 1971. The AEC carries a four compartment tank of 2500 gallons capacity and is shod on tubeless tyres. This model was arguably the finest four wheeler of its era and one of AEC's best designs.

Above: This is a fine study of a Volvo F86 tractor unit and semi trailer. It entered service in 1972. Of interest are the various notices emphasising the safety requirements and rules which must be adhered to by everyone entering the terminal.

Right: After the demise of the AEC marque in the late 1970s, Total switched to DAF for most of their transport needs. This photograph shows several models including DAF 2300 and DAF 2500 types. Whilst some of them were not the most powerful of vehicles, they were however, very reliable and economical to operate.

Left: Leyland Roadtrain rear steer six wheeled tractor unit and tandem axle semi-trailer. Total placed several of these units in service during the 1980s, this example, a later arrival, joining the fleet new in 1991. The tank capacity is 35,000 litres (7700 gallons).

Below: Total designed a new livery for their tankers in 1995 replacing the long-standing red and white cab style with single red 'TOTAL' on the front panel is in luminous paint and really stands out in darkness. DAF 85 series tractor units maintain the marque's presence in Total's fleet.

Wartime Pooling Arrangements

By the time of the Munich crisis in September 1938 it was apparent to many far sighted people that another war was inevitable. As a consequence, representatives of the four leading oil and petroleum distributors met with Government officials in 1938 to prepare for any such contingency.

The largest fuel retailers at the time were the Anglo-American Oil Company (Esso), National Benzole, Shell-Mex and B.P. and Trinidad Leaseholds (Regent). These companies along with thirty two other distributors formed the Petroleum and Lubricating Oil Boards when war was declared on 3rd September 1939. These committees were answerable to the Government's Oil Control Board.

The main activities of each company normally dictated which pooling board it joined. For instance, the Vacuum Oil Company (Mobil), then still a lubricants specialist, was one of the main constituents of the Lubricating Oil Board. However, some companies such as the Texas Oil Company, had representation on both boards. From the outset it was agreed that all resources should be 'pooled' for the common good. Hence the brand of 'Pool' petrol during the war and for a few years afterwards.

The Petroleum and Lubricating Oil Boards had to plan for greatly increased usage by the armed forces and industry. Apart from purely motive power needs, industrial demand for cutting oils and lubricants was to be huge. Private consumption had to be controlled by strict rationing and specially developed products such as high octane aviation spirit had to be allowed for. The boards had to be flexible and adaptable to respond to events and situations as they unfolded during the war years.

For example, by 1944 the RAF was using over 3 million gallons of aviation spirit during a single big raid over Germany. The USAAF would use a similar amount on a daylight raid. In 1939 the highest RAF estimates of aviation spirit requirements proved to be only one seventh of the actual consumption later in the war.

Another unforeseen event was the arrival of the American Forces in 1942. Their vehicles required leaded petrol and whilst this had been available for several years in Great Britain, demand was not great. To accommodate the Americans all grades were converted to leaded versions and this exercise involved emptying and re-supplying every petrol depot in the country.

At midnight on 3rd September 1939 about 18,500 people working for the oil companies in Britain came together into one huge organisation. All these companies pooled their assets including refineries, ocean going tankers, terminals, depots, installations and vehicles. Personnel who had been business rivals and competitors came together to work side by side in offices,

Right: When the Pool Petroleum Board came into being on September 3/4 1939 all the tankers from every oil company came under the new arrangements. Until the huge repainting programme was completed 'Pool' posters were affixed on to the tanks. This is a Dennis, FYK367, from the Shell-Mex and B.P. fleet.

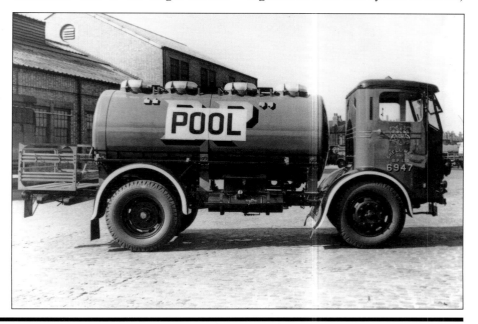

terminals and depots. There were no individual brands of petrol, just one 'pool' grade of each kind of product.

Below: A Leyland Hippo dating from circa 1935 in service with the Pool Board. Its tank and hose rack are battered but such vehicles were vital in the war years.

There were many difficulties to face as the war developed. The transportation of crude oil and refined products from overseas was the first one of these. There were, of course, refineries in Great Britain but it was also common practice to import refined products in bulk. Trinidad Leaseholds' refinery was vital in the Battle of Britain and when Japanese forces over-ran the Far Eastern oil installations later in the war, Anglo-Iranian's Abadan refinery managed to increase its output of vital aviation spirit.

The shortage of ocean going tankers became acute during the early years of war. They were always the prime targets in every convoy and there was a heavy loss of ships and crews. For a seaman to embark on a wartime voyage on a vessel laden with thousands of tons of high octane aviation spirit required a special kind of bravery.

In addition to attacks on tankers at sea, onshore refineries, terminals and installations were targeted by the Luftwaffe with several successes. The Royal Navy oil depot at Pembroke Dock was bombed in August 1940 and the resulting inferno raged for seventeen days.

Shell Haven was attacked in September 1940 as was Anglo-American's Purfleet terminal which was ablaze for several days. When Vacuum Oil's blending plant at Birkenhead was bombed the grease making department was destroyed. With grease being a vital lubricant for industry, emergency action had to be taken to resume production quickly and temporary accommodation was found in some nearby buildings which had been vacated by Anglo-American in the 1930s.

The logistics involved in transporting vast quantities of fuel and oil about the country were huge. The construction of airfields for the RAF and USAAF in East Anglia meant that massive tanker convoys were common sights on the narrow roads of, what was then, quite an isolated region.

The Americans brought their own road tankers with them and the British pool tanker fleet was supplemented with 'lease-lend' International lorries. Britain's largest heavy commercial vehicle manufacturers were engaged in war work and very few vehicles were available from them. However, new pool tankers were supplied in quantity by Bedford. Later in the war Maudslay was directed to build a quantity of lorries which were bodied as tankers.

One manufacturer which was no doubt very pleased to receive an order from the Ministry of Supply was Atkinson of Preston. This small company had been re-formed in 1933 after a period of financial difficulties. By 1940 they had only built a small number of vehicles but they were ordered to assemble 100 six wheeled tankers and 100 eight wheelers.

Wartime Pooling Arrangements

All these tankers joined the pool fleet and were fitted with AEC engines. Many of them continued in service with the oil companies until the late 1950s and helped to establish Atkinson's reputation as a builder of premium quality heavy vehicles.

Although peace returned in 1945 the pooling arrangements continued for several more years. Rationing remained in force and was not rescinded, for petrol, until May 1950.

The Pool Boards were de-merged on 30 June 1948 and the oil companies started to return to some semblance of normality and trading. All this took time and the common Pool brand of petrol was retained until 1953, although each company was able to re-introduce its own brand in 1952.

There can be no doubts that the Pool Petroleum and Lubricating Oil Boards did this country proud in the Second World War. The many difficulties faced and the vast quantities of products involved were unprecedented. The oil companies and their personnel responded in magnificent fashion to the challenge and the results achieved were object lessons in co-operation on a grand scale.

Top right: New vehicle were needed for the Pool fleet and with the larger premium quality makers such as Leyland and AEC fully committed to war munitions and vehicle manufacture, lighter, mass produced chassis were used as tankers. This Bedford O-type was one of hundreds of the model supplied during the war years.

Above right and right: Every British lorry builder contributed to the war effort in some way. Atkinson of Preston was one of the smallest commercial vehicle assemblers and the order they received for one hundred six wheelers and one hundred eight wheelers from the Pool Board was far more than they had built since the firm was re-formed in 1933. All had AEC 7.7 litre engines; the six wheelers received 3000 gallon tanks and the eight wheelers 3600 gallon tanks. Note the white edged mudguards and masked headlights for the blackout. Convoys of Pool tankers supplied numerous airfields during the night.

Above: The shortage of suitable vehicles from British makers caused the Pool Board to use several International tankers built in the USA and supplied under the 'lease-lend' agreement. They were a heavyweight design and many of them continued to work well after the war had ended.

Right: One of the numerous Scammells which came from the oil companies into the Pool fleet on the outbreak of war. This fuel oil tanker previously serving in the colours of the Anglo-American Oil Company (Esso).

Above: The Leyland Lynx model was still in production in 1941 at Leyland's Kingston factory. A semi-forward control design, it had been first introduced in 1935 designed for a 5 ton payload but with a low unladen weight. The model could be specified to be fitted with either a petrol or diesel engine.

Left: Dennis was one of the lorry builders with sufficient capacity to be able to provide some vehicles to the Pool Board. This Max has a three compartment tank of 1500 gallons capacity. Note the tarpaulins and damaged roof on the buildings. Was this caused by bombing raids?

Right: In the immediate post-war period manufacturers were still beset with numerous problems and shortages of raw materials. There was a desperate need for new vehicles in every sector of road transport. New tankers were ordered by the Pool Board and Maudslay received a large order for their Mogul Mk.2 model. The standard engine was the AEC 7.7 litre unit with the option of a Gardner 5LW. The coachbuilt cab was utilitarian and most had three compartment tanks of 1500 gallons capacity fitted.

Left: During the period from the end of the war in 1945 until the dissolution of the Pool Boards in 1948, the oil companies were allowed to discreetly display their names on vehicles. References to Pool have been painted out on this 1930s Bedford WHL laden with lubricants from an Anglo-American depot.

Below: Relatively small numbers of Thornycroft Trusty eight wheelers were ordered by the Pool Board in the last couple of years of its existence. This example is equipped with a twin compartment tank of 3000 gallons capacity for diesel and light fuel oils. Fina operated some of these Thornycrofts after the dissolution of the Pool Board.

Above: Scammell supplied many articulated eight wheelers to the Pool Boards. The fleet no. reveals that this example was purchased directly by the Board as opposed to being part of a requisitioned fleet. The tank has a capacity of 3000 gallons. The photograph was taken in the early post-war period.

Road Tanker & Fuel Terminal Operations

A modern fuel delivery tanker is an expensive and sophisticated piece of equipment. It has to be used efficiently and its daily workload planned meticulously.

Each major oil company operates a series of strategically located distribution sites and these are usually near to the larger population centres. One or two petroleum producers do not market their products nationally but all the oil companies co-operate through exchange arrangements.

These agreements vary depending upon the partners involved; they might take the form of two or more companies sharing a terminal or, alternatively, exchanges of products take place at other terminals. This allows tankers to re-load at convenient depots without the need for returning empty to their home bases. Such arrangements improve tanker utilisation and efficiency.

The Nottingham Terminal of Total Oil Great Britain Ltd is a modern and efficiently run operation and the following information provides an insight into how a busy distribution network is controlled. This particular terminal is supplied nightly by train from Lindsey Oil Refinery and an average load is 2000 tonnes. In a typical week nine such loads are received.

Other oil companies supply some terminals by pipeline directly from refineries and some facilities located at ports or with river access are supplied by coastal tankers. One or two are still dependent upon inland waterways for their products.

Returning to Nottingham and once the train has been positioned in the sidings, Total's employees start unloading it. The contents of each rail tank are pumped to the tank farm at the terminal where a variety of petroleum products are stored. The control room directs the fuels to their correct storage tanks and once the train has been unloaded the pipeline is purged to remove residual vapour. Fuel excise duty is charged by Customs & Excise immediately it leaves the refinery so storage quantities are kept to safe minimum levels.

Total's Nottingham Terminal operates from early Monday morning until mid-day Saturday and the tankers are double shifted. All are now maximum capacity 38 tonnes gross train weight vehicles and on average 150-160 loads of fuel are dispatched daily. Not all of these leave in Total's tankers; other oil companies, distributors and hauliers are continuously collecting loads.

Total's drivers work alternating weekly day and night shifts and

Nottingham also controls a number of tankers and drivers based at terminals owned by Gulf Oil at West Bromwich and Esso at Birmingham. Typically the tankers average 2500 km weekly and each round trip averages 95-100km. That is laden from terminal to customer and returning to collect another load which could be from another company's depot.

Customer orders are received at a central order office which places them with the appropriate terminal. Orders are processed on a 48 hour cycle - for instance, those received before 5.00 pm Monday will be fulfilled Wednesday.

There are seasonal fluctuations in demand with wintertime causing heating oils to be used in greater quantity. In the summer months petrol sales increase and these variations affect tanker utilisation. In extremely busy periods third party hauliers are hired.

It is vital that careful planning is given to every load. Petroleum products vary in density and therefore weight. Whilst a 38 tonnes gtw tanker can legally carry 36,000 litres of petrol (7900 gallons) the same vehicle can only carry 30,000 litres (6600 gallons) of gas oil. Allocation of quantities to each tanker compartment is necessary to avoid axle overloads and potential stability problems. If mixed loads of petrol and derv are carried it is essential that the load quantities are carefully calculated.

Modern tankers are designed to take into account any future gross weight increases and have capacities of 39,000 litres. Generally they have six compartments of between 6000 and 7000 litres each and are usually mounted on tri-axle semi-trailers, these being more manoeuvrable than tandem axle types. On the motive power front, the older three-axle tractive units are being phased out.

The office staff at the terminal programme all the details of a load into the computer and prepare the paperwork for the tanker driver. Each driver has an individual card which identifies him and his vehicle to the security system. Loading cannot commence until a certain procedure has been followed and the appropriate checks made. When the driver is ready to load he must enter the amounts of fuel for each of the tanker's compartments into the correct pump's meters. If this information agrees with that already in the computer, loading will commence providing that the tanker has been earthed.

All modern tankers are now bottom loaders, this process being cleaner, safer for the driver and quicker to fill. They incorporate overload prevention and anti spill devices and, because they are sealed systems, vapour recovery is part of the process when they are being filled.

When loaded the driver proceeds to the exit gate, identifies himself to the system and receives a bill of lading for his load. He can then start his journey. All Total's tankers are equipped with cab phones so that contact between the driver and his base is possible at any time. In the near future it is probable that tankers will carry computer terminals for printing delivery notes.

When a new service station site is being planned or an existing one re-developed, careful consideration is given to tanker access and the location of the discharge point. It is a requirement that in the event of any incident the tanker must be able to leave the site quickly without having to reverse or shunt in any way.

Down the years both filling station sites and tankers have become much

Above: During the first quarter of the century much of this country's oil requirements were imported in refined grades. Anglo-American imported huge quantities and this was the scene in May 1921 at their Ocean Terminal, Mode Wheel. After unloading ocean going tankers the products are transferred to rail and road tankers. Shown in the photograph are three steam wagons for fuel oil transportation and the shunting engine 'Powerful' with a train of lamp oil tank-cars.

Right: A good example of top loading from an uncovered rack. It is Freeth Street, Nottingham in July 1948 and the time of the dissolution of the Petroleum Pool Board. All three tankers are in Pool livery with Fina identified on the tank of the Austin nearest the camera. The others are a Dennis and Morris Commercial.

larger. It is recalled that when several brands of petrol were sold from one forecourt individual delivery quantities were small. When these same retailers switched to solus trading their storage capacity was such that twice daily deliveries were not uncommon.

Also in those years there were many small tankers of 2000 to 2700 gallons (9000 - 12,300 litres) capacity. Nowadays an average service station will receive at least two deliveries weekly. Typically these will be full loads of about 34,000 litres (7500 gallons) and they are normally mixed tankers containing both petrol and derv.

One of the prime considerations in operating terminals and road tankers is safety. Petrol tankers have always been divided into compartments so that in the event of the tank being ruptured in an accident only part of the contents will be spilled.

In the event of severe winter weather the terminal managers can make a decision to suspend deliveries until conditions improve.

Historically it is interesting to note that for many years the Carriage of Petroleum Regulations decreed that the maximum compartment size was 800 gallons (3630 litres). This was the size of the very first lorry tanker built by Anglo-American (Esso) in 1905. As lorries have become bigger, particularly in the last thirty years or so, tank compartment sizes have been increased to today's maximum of 7500 litres (1650 gallons).

Tanker drivers must have an ADR Certificate which is only awarded after attending a course on the transportation of hazardous goods. Thereafter they must re-sit the examination every five years and Total's staff attend interim courses every two years. All terminal staff and drivers are trained in fire-fighting techniques.

Driver training in all aspects of the job is important and for many years some oil companies have supported the annual Lorry Driver of the Year Contest. Every year regional heats are held with the winners from each depot going through to the National Final. Many companies also make awards to their

drivers with safe and accident free records.

The quest for even better tanker utilisation and efficiency is on-going and Driver Controlled Deliveries (DCD) are becoming more widespread. These can be applied to 'out of hours' deliveries. Presently, night shift drivers are restricted to supplying late opening service stations, authorised distributors and industrial customers. Traditionally, at filling stations the driver must be accompanied by one other person at all times during discharging. With the DCD scheme the tanker driver is able to make the delivery on his own. There are certain procedures to be adhered to which must satisfy the local Petroleum Officer and night-time deliveries to sites in residential areas will not be considered because of potential noise intrusion.

Serious incidents involving road tankers are extremely rare and this is as a result of the safety rules applied to every stage of the process involving equipment and people. Safety is the over-riding consideration at all times and the oil industry's distribution network is run on very safe and efficient lines. These systems have evolved during the last century and the oil companies operate a transport and distribution network which is a role model for lorry operators everywhere.

Author's note:
Many of the procedures for operating road tankers described in this chapter are specific to Total Oil Great Britain Ltd and its Nottingham Terminal in particular. However, they are representative of similar terminals and tanker fleets operated by all the large British oil companies featured in this book.

Right: This is an intriguing photograph from the mid 1950s of Fina's Grangemouth Terminal. Other photographs show that the far end of this depot was enclosed, so how did the tankers get in and out? A wonderful selection of period vehicles. Several Bedfords ranging from 1930s to 1950s, Morris Leader, two Austins, AEC Monarch and possibly a Leyland Lynx. Not forgetting the Fordson van, Standard Eight car and is that a Morris car in the centre?

A very simple loading system which can service both road and rail tankers. Note the chain pulls for the valve in the control of the driver and the man on the gantry is about to tie up the filling hose. The Bedford S-type articulated fuel oil tanker dates from the early 1950s and it is just apparent that the discharge valves, etc. are housed in a separate rear compartment.

Above: Early 1960's view of the extensive Shell-Mex and B.P. vehicle workshops at Wandsworth. In the foreground are a pair of Leyland Beaver 2000 gallon capacity tankers in the green Power Petroleum Company livery and alongside is a 2500 gallon AEC Mercury. In the background is one of the Rolls Royce 88R petrol engined ERF 4000 gallon eight wheelers.

Right: Another early 1960s scene - this featuring the spacious terminal at Colwick on the outskirts of Nottingham. Fina and Regent were neighbours and the Fina AEC Mercury tractor unit and single axle semi-trailer have easy access and exit to and from the covered loading rack.

Above and right: Two views from 1963 featuring one of the large capacity loading racks at the Shell-Mex and B.P. terminal at Wandsworth and capable of accommodating eight tankers at any one time. An AEC Mercury, a Scammell Highwayman and a Leyland Comet together with a S20 Foden of Golders Green-based A. Pannell fill-up for another delivery. On another occasion an AEC Mammoth Major Mk.V heads up a line which also includes a Leyland Beaver and an elderly Scammell 'Artic Eight' unit.

Left: A representative selection of the Shell-Mex and B.P. Heathrow refuelling fleet at its airfield fuel rack in the 1960s. The Bedford J type is equipped with a 300 gallon tank, its drawbar trailer's - longer but narrower - tank also having a capacity of 300 gallons. Vehicles such as these were necessary to service the ever-growing executive traffic making use of the airport's facilities. Other vehicles include examples of the impressive AEC Mk.V powered 'Yorkshire' refueller, having a capacity of 10,000 gallons, Leyland 'Hippo' powered 'Cornwall' drawbar units - each having a capacity of 7,800 gallons and a Foden powered 'Hertford' refueller of 3425 gallons.

Road Tanker & Terminal Operations

Above: This is the Lindsey Oil Refinery of Fina and Total on Humberside as seen in the early 1970s. The tanker parking area in the foreground is a delight for connoisseurs of the classic British lorry. In evidence are Scammells, Atkinsons, Guys and AECs liveried for Fina, Total, Mobil and Gulf. Furthermore, in the bottom right hand corner of the photograph, an ERF of Smith and Robinson is pulling on to the weighbridge and under the distant loading rack far right is another AEC and a Leyland. What memories. What nostalgia.

Left: Drive-under covered loading rack with the various products available in each bay clearly displayed. This was a typical Esso installation of the early 1970s with Leyland Beaver and AEC Mandator articulated tankers loading up.

Top Right: All the oil companies use a common colour coded method of pipework identification for their various products. Also incorporated into bottom loading is vapour recovery; the narrower pipe nearest the camera. Most bottom loaders can also be filled from on top and have dipping facility for customers who still demand it. Eventually top loading tankers will be phased out.

Middle Right: A big advance in loading procedures came with the introduction of bottom loading tankers in the mid 1980s. Until then top loading had been the norm since the first days of tankers. Bottom loading is safer and cleaner for the driver and also quicker.

Right: The sidings alongside Total's Leeds terminal. Not all sidings are adjacent to a terminal and in instances where this occurs a short pipeline is necessary.

Road Tanker & Terminal Operations

Above: Most oil refineries have at least one shunting engine for internal duties and assembling trains of tank-cars for Railfreight to take to the terminals. Oil trains usually run during the night to take advantage of cheaper freight rates.

Left and below left: Safety is of paramount importance at all terminals and installations. All drivers and staff are trained in fire fighting and containment techniques and foam tankers are based at all terminals in case of an emergency. Here are two examples of Total foam tankers based on a DAF 2500 artic and AEC Mammoth Major eight wheeler.

Below: Exercises in safe procedures also take place at regular intervals and here staff are being trained in the procedure of unloading an overturned tanker by pumping the contents into an adjacent empty example.

Above: Traditionally it has been a requirement that all deliveries to service stations must be supervised by one other person in addition to the tanker driver. This is now changing with the introduction of driver controlled deliveries. This scene dates from May 1970 with a 1968 AEC Mammoth Major six wheeler tractor unit on super single tyres. The tandem axle semi-trailer is similarly shod.

Right: Many customers still insist on seeing the dips when a load of petrol and diesel is delivered despite accurately metered and measured loading procedures. The lorry is a 1992 ERF E10 rear steer six wheeler tractor unit and it is unloading in a spacious area with excellent access.

Road Tanker & Terminal Operations

Left: This photograph gives a fine contrast with the previous one showing a delivery which nowadays would be frowned upon. The AEC Mandator tanker is tight against the fence and is unable to leave the site without shunting in the event of an emergency. There is in fact plenty of room for a re-design of the delivery point to overcome the problem and have the tanker face an unrestricted exit point. This photograph was taken in the mid 1970s.

Below: Another view of the modern method with individual storage tank filling valves located together in a row, rather than on top of each tank, with access through a metal cover. The tanker has nothing in front or behind it. ERF E12TX two-axle tractor unit with tri-axle semi-trailer, new in 1992.

Above: Various styles and designs of tankers have been seen over the years. The traditional cylindrical shape was adapted from the earliest days and has remained basically unchanged to the present time. This mid 1950s AEC Mammoth Major Eight Mk.III has received a fully enclosed tank; very innovative at the time.

Right: A Regent tanker from the early 1950s with fairings and rear covering. The vehicle is probably a Dennis and it is recalled that the hoses could work their way to the front of the enclosed rack making it difficult to retrieve them if they were not securely fastened.

Right: A simpler style of fairings used on several makes of articulated tanker. This one was made by Steel Barrel Company and the AEC Mercury dates from 1955. Tank capacity is 3000 gallons.

Road Tanker & Terminal Operations

Right: Because they have been such large fleet operators the oil companies have been at the forefront of lorry design and innovation. This AEC Mandator Mk.V tractor unit is fitted with an experimental fifth wheel coupling for its semi-trailer. The tank is a twin compartment design for diesel and light fuel oils and it was new in 1961.

Above: Stability has always been a very important consideration in tanker design. This AEC Mandator was taking part in a series of tests to measure stability and the differences between the influences of single and twin rear wheels. Various suspension settings were also used in these experiments conducted by the Road Research Laboratories and Texaco. The tanker capacity is 6300 gallons.

Right: A low centre of gravity will obviously give improved stability and Charles Roberts designed and introduced lower tankers in the 1980s. Here the differences in height are apparent between the standard design on the left and the new one. The location is at the front of BP's London headquarters.

Above: The oil companies have encouraged safe and courteous driving from their drivers for many years. In the early 1920s Vacuum Oil displayed such notices on the tail-boards of their lorries. The vehicle is a 1920 AEC Y-type.

Left: The annual Lorry Driver of the Year contest has always been well supported by the oil companies and their drivers. This photograph taken at the finals of the 1963 competition shows a Scammell Highwayman artic operated by one of Mobil's authorised distributors attempting one of the tests.

Road Tanker & Terminal Operations

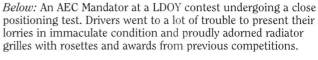

Below: A LDOY regional heat held in the late 1960s. An Atkinson Mk.II eight wheeler is carefully reversed in one of the tests. Remember, such vehicles rarely had power assisted steering in those days so such manoeuvres were not easy.

Below: An AEC Mandator at a LDOY contest undergoing a close positioning test. Drivers went to a lot of trouble to present their lorries in immaculate condition and proudly adorned radiator grilles with rosettes and awards from previous competitions.

Left: A LDOY competition held in 1960 at Oxford. An attentive audience watches as a AEC Mammoth Major Mk.III eight wheeler in Mobilgas livery, but operated by Home Counties Petroleum Products, tackles one of the reversing tests. A BRS Commer undertakes another reversing test in the background. Note also the Leyland Beavers with Hillman car bodies from the Pressed Steel Company for delivery to the Rootes Group.

Right: A good example of the precise positioning required in the reversing tests at a LDOY contest. The AEC Mammoth Minor twin steer tractor unit was new to Conoco/Jet in 1967.

Above: In addition to contests such as LDOY, oil company tankers have featured in numerous trade shows, processions and carnivals. After all, a well presented vehicle is a good marketing tool and prominent advertisement for a company. Driver N A Hughes proudly stands alongside his Leyland Octopus 24.04 which won first prize and a highly commended at Bootle Carnival on 16 July 1963. The tanker was on contract to Fina and operated by Lawrensons.

Right: Another proud driver and his trophy - unfortunately his name is not recorded - after winning his class at the English Riviera Concours d'Elegance at Paignton in the 1960s. The tanker, a Morris seven-tonner, was operated by Western Petroleum Products of Plymouth.

Petrol Retailing & Service Stations

When motor cars first appeared on the roads, service stations did not exist. Petrol was sold in two gallons capacity cans from a variety of outlets such as blacksmiths, ironmongers and even chemists.

Before very long the garage trade evolved to sell, service and repair cars as well as retailing petrol. Because of its volatility and flammable characteristics, regulations for the safe storage of petrol were soon introduced. Petrol continued to be sold in cans for many years despite the first kerbside pump being introduced in 1919. Early petrol pumps were mechanically operated. Then some types worked on a syphon principle and, finally, the electrically powered pumps so familiar today were perfected. Examples of the original types of mechanical pumps survived in rural areas until well into the 1950s.

As the number of available petrol brands increased, garage and service station owners started to sell several varieties and photographs exist of sites which offered motorists a choice from at least nine different brands of petrol.

In the 1920s and 30s brand loyalty was very strong and much of the advertising aimed at motorists was connected with record breaking achievements of one sort or another such as speed and endurance. In the 1920s and until the mid 1930s if a filling station was offering just one petrol brand it was probably owned by that company. When Trinidad Leaseholds with Regent started to expand, it persuaded the first service station proprietors to switch to solus trading, that is selling just one brand of petrol.

The change to solus trading gathered pace in the 1950s when brands were marketed again after the period of Pool petrol and rationing. Other companies such as Mobil and Jet entered the marketplace, although Jet tended to concentrate on smaller sites, increasing sales through price cutting. By 1970 solus trading was the norm and other subtle changes had also taken place.

In 1960 the typical service station consisted of three or four pumps offering a choice of 95, 97 and 100 octane petrol. There would also be a service bay for car repairs and servicing. The site owner might also have a side-line in second-hand car dealing and the kiosk might have offered a few items of sugar confectionery and cigarettes.

Service would have been provided by an attendant and engine oil was sold in glass bottles which were re-filled by the staff. Unless the site was alongside a busy main road it would not open before 8.00 am and close in the early evening. Typically motorists asked for a specific number of gallons and never filled their car's petrol tank more than half full unless going on holiday.

By 1970 further changes were taking place as self service pumps were introduced. This necessitated in forecourts being rebuilt to include a canopy and provide more space. Gradually the service station of today evolved with its focus purely on petrol retailing and a convenience shop. A wide range of products are available and many sites are open from early morning until late at night, with 24 hours opening becoming more common. To refurbish an average sized site can cost up to £500,000 and it is usual to sell three grades of petrol and one of diesel.

At the time of writing there are approximately 15,000 service stations in Great Britain. Probably 45% of this total are owned by the oil companies and several are also managed by them. Many sites, however, are run by independent operators including sole traders, limited companies and partnerships. In addition there are 60 or so motorway service areas and almost 600 filling stations attached to supermarkets.

These have taken an ever increasing share of the petrol market in the last decade as they have undercut other retailers on price and as a consequence forced many independents out of business. However, having achieved a significant share of the market, their pump prices are now not necessarily the lowest, and more often than not merely reflect the local average pump price.

Interestingly the price of petrol in real terms is slightly less than it was in 1960, and considerably less than in 1980. The significant difference is that in 1960 just over 50% of the price paid by the motorist went to the government in taxation. Nowadays over 70% of the purchase price is tax.

During the last 35 years petrol service stations have changed out of all recognition. Now there are fewer brands available and the sites tend to concentrate on the requirements of the motorist rather than the needs of his or her vehicle - that is apart from the obvious one of fuel to provide the means of propulsion.

Right: Many early service stations came into being as offshoots of other businesses. Hardisty and Miller were coal merchants as well as petrol retailers. There is plenty of advertising for Pratts spirit on display and three early types of pump and the rear of a tanker. This photograph dates from the early 1920s.

Below: The Car Mart, Edgware Road, London and a fine array of typical 1920s style petrol pumps. The brands on sale are Redline, Pratts, Shell and National Benzole. Note the fire extinguishers and sand buckets.

Left: This 1930s photograph of Burnley Bros, Manningham Lane, Bradford shows a typical service station of the period. Petrol brands on sale are Power, Shell, Shell-Mex, National Benzole, Cleveland and B.P. Mobiloil lubricants are also advertised and note the white coated attendants. Power petrol costs one shilling and tuppence a gallon (6p) and motor oil five old pence a pint (2p). The good old days!

Petrol Retailing & Service Stations

Right: This is something of a mystery photograph borrowed from Fina. The lady is identified as Florrie Ford, a famous music hall star in the first half of the century. The car is a Renault and it is being filled with Zip petrol, the brand of Russian Oil Products. R.O.P was taken over by Regent after the war and Vic Allen confirmed that this was definitely a R.O.P depot; the corrugated iron fence is the clue. Probable date of the scene is late 1930s.

Below: Northway Garage, Hendon in the late 1930s and National Benzole's Thornycroft tanker makes a delivery. In addition to National the garage is selling Cleveland, Esso and Shell brands of petrol.

Above: This is quite a large forecourt for the 1950s with lots of space and a cashiers cabin. Eight B.P. pumps in total with quite a variation in grade prices: Regular at 4s 3d (21p), Super at 4s 9d (23.5p) and Super-plus at 5s (25p). A difference of 9d (3.5p) was significant in 1959, the date of this photograph. The location is Bagshot, Surrey.

Left: This is a nice early 1950s view of a typical rural service station. It was owned by K Parkyn, Helsington Garage on the A6 near Kendal. Then the road was a busy main trunk route. The pumps are all Fina grades and Mobiloil and B.P. lubricants are available.

Petrol Retailing & Service Stations

Right: Two Guy Big J artics of Regent making the first deliveries of the brand to Bloody Oaks Service Station, Stamford, in 1967. Note that in place of the usual 'Regent' roundels on the tanker cabs they are carrying posters of Caroline, the Regent cowgirl introduced in 1965. Her slogan "ride Regent, the lively one". Where is she now? Period cars are an Austin Westminster and Jaguar Mk.X.

Below: By the late 1960s self service stations were becoming quite common and trading stamps were on offer at many sites to tempt customers. The petrol retailing trade was becoming even more competitive. This is Wigan Lane service station, Wigan, circa 1969.

Above: One idea which never caught on was the mobile filling station. Introduced in 1964 by European Petroleum Distributors Ltd., it was proposed to take petrol to the motorist at large gatherings such as race meetings. Based on an AEC Mammoth Major Eight Mk.V, it had a 4000 gallons capacity tank built by Darham Industries.

Below: Texaco's latest style and design of service station in the 1990s. The ERF E12TX articulated tanker is about to make its delivery.

Above: BP introduced the Truck-Stop concept to Great Britain in the 1980s specifically for heavy goods vehicle drivers. They provide a very high standard of catering and cleanliness and are well patronised by drivers. They also sell large quantities of diesel, discharged through high speed pumps to cope with the large fuel tanks on modern lorries.

Road Tankers & Service Stations in Colour

Above: This immaculately restored AEC Mercury four compartment tanker in Shell-Mex and B.P. livery dates from 1957. Owned by BP, it was photographed in August 1987 at the Lorry Driver of the Year finals which were being held at Cranfield, Bedfordshire that year.

Below: The Leyland Octopus 24.04 was one of the classic eight wheelers of the 1950s, numerous examples being operated by Shell-Mex and B.P. They also had some memorable liveries; well illustrated by this fine photograph. The tank is of 4000 gallons capacity having six compartments.

Above: This ERF EC10 rear steer six wheeler tractor unit and tandem axle semi-trailer photographed in the Scottish Highlands in August 1995, entered service with the company during the previous year. BP's future vehicle purchasing policy will probably be to revert to tri-axle semi-trailers in anticipation of future gross train weight increases and the corresponding tank capacity increases from the present 36,000 litres to an anticipated 39,000 litres.

Right: After the Conoco take-over of Jet Petroleum in 1961 several tankers were painted in the cherry red livery of Conoco. This is an AEC Mammoth Major Mk.V eight wheeler with a six compartment 4000 gallons tank. This photograph dates from 1964 and by then lorry fuel tanks were mounted on the off-side. Note the dipsticks on top of the tanker, and the spare wheel and carrier is an unusual feature. They were normally removed to save weight and discourage theft.

Below: ERF became a popular make in many oil company fleets in the 1980s, and this E10 tractor unit was new in 1989. Then, the rear steer six wheeler tractor and tandem axle trailer was considered the optimum configuration to maximise payload within the 38 tonnes gross train weight limit. Typically the tank capacity is 35,000 litres (7750 gallons).

Above: The Leyland Gas Turbine Truck was designed to operate at 38 tons gtw and at speeds of up to 70 mph. Claimed benefits included cleaner exhaust emissions, reduced noise, quicker acceleration, lower fuel consumption and cheaper maintenance costs. Then, however, Britain's roads were not a place where the vehicle's efficiency could be fully exploited - diesel fuel was cheap and the Ergomatic-cabbed vehicle never went into production.

Above: Leyland Octopus 24.O4 eight wheeler loading product at a terminal, in the background is a Bedford TK articulated unit. This photograph illustrates the mainly red livery employed by Esso in the 1950s and early 1960s.

Below: This Scammell Handyman artic was photographed in Luton in June 1970, having just made a delivery of fuel oil to the Vauxhall car plant. The Handyman Mk.1 had a wheelbase of 8ft 6in and was superseded by the Michelotti-cabbed Handyman 2 in 1965.

Above: In recent times, the Scania product has found favour in the Esso fleet and soon after the launch of the 4-Series, examples began appearing in the company's livery. This unit was photographed in April 1998 whilst making a delivery to the service station on the M5 Exeter services.

Left: What might be described as traditional sites - that is without canopies and with attended service - were becoming less common in the 1980s. In this photograph an Esso ERF C40 maximum capacity tanker is about to make a delivery to such a location.

Right: AEC Mercury tractor unit new in 1963 coupled to a four-compartment fuel oil semi-trailer. The trailer design of twin oscillating axles, more commonly known as 'four-in-line', was a popular design of the period. Mercurys had a variety of design gross train weights for articulated use; 18, 22 or 24 tons depending upon the rear axle fitted. From the type of trailer being used this is probably a 22 tons gtw version.

Above: Seddon Atkinson 4-11 rear steer six wheeler tractor unit and tandem axle semi-trailer. It entered service with Fina in 1987, the six-compartment tank having a capacity of 36,000 litres.

Right: This brand new Mercedes 1834 shows off the new Fina livery to good effect. The unit was photographed making a delivery to the Watling Street Cafe on the A5 near Flamstead in August 1994.

This fine photograph dates from 1960/61 and is of an Albion Caledonian newly into service painted in Gulf's orange and blue livery of the period. The tanker is for bulk oil deliveries, although Gulf petrol was about to be another new brand on the market at the time. The Albion was a contract vehicle operated by Gilbraith Tankers of Accrington.

Left: ERF was Britain's last remaining independent lorry manufacturer able to offer a complete range of heavy vehicles. By the 1990s they had established a strong presence in the fleets of most major oil companies. This EC10 model was new in 1996 and it is coupled to a Thompson Carmichael '5500' tanker semi-trailer. This is a new design jointly developed by the tank manufacturer, Gulf and Tankfreight.

Below: Leyland 'Power Plus' Beaver and four-in-line semi-trailer. This model was introduced in 1961, the LAD cab only being used for about three years on Leyland's premium range. The 4000 gallon capacity tank semi-trailer was a design used almost exclusively by Mobil and probably was the most economical method of obtaining the maximum 24 ton gross train weight applicable at the time. The photograph dates from July 1963, the location being the M6 near Charnock Richard, Lancs.

Above: Latest additions to Mobil's fleet in 1995 included a batch of ERF EC10 rear steer tractor units. This example being photographed outside of Mobil's new head office at Milton Keynes.

Right: This Leyland Octopus 24.0/4 tanker was about to join the Shell road tanker fleet, delivering lubricants to power plants and transformer stations, when photographed in 1960. The Butterfield 4000 gallon single compartment mild steel road tank was lined with 'Epikote', a resin based paint manufactured by the Shell Chemical Co. Ltd.

Road Tankers in Colour

Left: Leyland Hippo 'Cornwall' six wheeler and drawbar trailer used for airport refuelling duties. The gross train weight for this outfit, 56 tons, restricted it to airfields, hence there being no requirement to register it for use on public roads. Whilst this is very much a specialist vehicle equipped with heavy pumping equipment, it is interesting to note that the same capacity (7800 gallons) is now conveyed by artic tankers within the current 38 tonnes limit. Such has been the improvement in chassis and tank design and the use of composite materials. The dramatic photograph was taken in the winter of 1962/3.

Below: In the mid 1950s the rigid eight wheeler was flagship in any road transport fleet. Shell-Mex and B.P. operated hundreds of such vehicles as tankers and AEC Mammoth Major Eight Mk.IIIs were one of the most popular type. This six compartment tank of 4000 gallons capacity and indeed the complete vehicle has a superb livery. The distinctive sliding door cab is by Reeve and Kenning.

A Century of Petroleum Transport

Right: Albion Caledonian eight wheelers were not used in anything like the numbers as similar chassis supplied by Leyland and AEC to Shell-Mex and B.P. However, quite a few were cabbed by Alfred Miles as an option to the Leyland structure more commonly used on such Albions. This was a striking livery for the period and the tanker's capacity was 3600 gallons. The photograph dates from the late 1950s.

Below: The prominent Shell livery of yellow, white and red has remained basically unchanged for approximately 40 years. It dates back to the Shell-Mex and B.P. era and though subtle variations have taken place in the intervening years it is recognisable from that period. The Foden 4350 rear steer tractor unit was new in 1992. It is coupled to a tandem axle tank semi-trailer of 35,000 litres capacity.

Above: Regent had one of the most outstanding liveries of the 1950s; navy blue, red and white with 'Regent' in gold. This Leyland Octopus 22.O1 was new in the early 1950s and has a 3600 gallon five compartment tank.

Left: Texaco had operated very few, if any, six wheeled tankers since their last rear steer AEC Mercury conversions in the early 1970s. However, In 1982 the type was again to find favour with the company when the decision was made to purchase a number of three-axle Leyland Constructors. This example has a five compartment tank specifically for delivering diesel fuel.

Right: Wincanton took over the Texaco contract for distribution in 1991 and introduced ERF tractor units. This Rolls Royce Eagle TX powered model with tri-axle semi-trailer is pictured in front of Texaco's new offices at Canary Wharf in 1992, very close to Prince Regent's Wharf which was the home of Burt, Boulton and Haywood to whom the present day Texaco can trace its origins in this country.

Below: In the mid 1990s Total purchased a large batch of ERF tractor units. They have reverted to the configuration of a two axle unit and tri-axle semi-trailer in anticipation of future gross weight increases. Also such an articulated outfit has been found to be more manoeuvrable than a 3+2 combination. Tank capacity is 39,000 litres (8580 gallons) although the present weight limits restrict this to 36,000 litres (7900 gallons) of petrol.

Service Stations in Colour

Left: This was quite an innovative service station in the 1960s, it being mainly constructed of plastic materials. Two of the pumps are multi-grade dispensers and a total of five grades are available. Petrol was sold by its octane rating for quite a lengthy period and the dual star system. From the multi-pumps 91, 93, 95, 97 and 99 octanes are available with a separate pump for 101 octane petrol. The site was Baldock, Herts in June 1968.

Below: Typical 1980s development of a service station site close to a roundabout, always a good location. Prominent and with good access. A Leyland Roadtrain articulated tanker leaves after making a delivery.

Left: A large site typical of new developments in the 1980s and 1990s providing plenty of room and excellent access for all sizes of vehicles, ranging from private cars to tankers and other heavy goods vehicles.

Right: Night-time shot of BP's level five service station at Pitlochry in September 1995. Compared with the photographs of forecourts taken 60 and 70 years ago what a difference there is. The basic commodity of petrol is still used for propulsion as it was then, but the means of distributing it and retailing have changed greatly over the years.

Below: The latest forecourt design and layout adopted by Fina in the 1990s. Careful planning goes into all aspects of a modern service station to maximise the space available and to present a clean and easily identifiable image.

Photographic Credits & Picture Index

The vast majority of the photographs in this book have been obtained from the relevant oil company featured. In some cases these were commissioned from a professional photographer, and where appropriate, the studio or photographer has been acknowledged. In all cases permission has been given by the relevant company for their archive material to be used. In some instances, where the copyright was doubtful, every effort has been made to trace the photographer. Sometimes, because of the age of the material, that has proved to be impossible.

Photographs credited to 'AEC' are from the large collection in the care of the AEC Society, obtained by them from various sources, the negatives of which are believed to be held by the BCVM Trust Archives.

AEC: 100, 122, 131

V. Allen Collection: 87, 88, 89, 121, 122, 144
V. Allen/Butterfields: 85
V. Allen/Northern Aluminium: 85
V. Allen/Vauxhall Motors: 86/87
V. Allen/Ford Motor Company: 87
V. Allen/Gloster Saro: 90/91

BP: 8/9, 10, 11, 12/13, 12, 14, 15, 69, 70/71, 71, 76, 77, 80, 78, 81, 102, 104, 105, 106, 107, 122, 127, 128, 129, 131, 132, 133, 142, 143, 146, 147

Conoco: 5, 16/17, 18, 19, 20, 21, 22, 23, 119
Conoco/A. Bloomfield: 134, 146
Conoco/Burton: 134

Peter Davies: 33, 132, 135, 137, 141
M. Doherty: 100, 101, 118

Esso: 25, 26, 28/29, 32, 33, 34, 35, 116, 127, 135, 136

Fina: 37, 39, 43, 44, 45, 46, 47, 109, 110/111, 111, 112/113, 125, 128, 136, 137, 147
Fina/GGS: 47
Fina/H.J. Hare: 38, 43, 45, 130
Fina/Lincoln: 37, 38, 39, 40/41
Fina/Marshall: 114
Fina/Northgate: 42
Fina/Romney: 42
Fina/Stewart Bale: 129

Gulf: 49, 53, 118
Gulf/R. Savage ABIPP: 53, 117
Gulf/Williams: 140

Arthur Ingram Collection: 5, 6, 7, 11, 14, 19, 25, 26/27, 29, 30/31, 32, 50, 65, 67, 68/69, 69, 70, 72, 73, 76, 77, 79, 80, 81, 82, 83, 103, 104, 106, 107, 109, 121, 125, 135, 138/139

J. Kimp/Shell: 2/3, 7, 69, 74/75, 76, 78, 79, 80, 82, 114, 115

David Lee: 136
Leyland Truck & Bus: 46

Mobil: Cover picture, 55, 58, 59, 60, 61, 62, 63, 119, 121, 123, 124, 125, 140, 141
Mobil/Hutchins & Moore: 59
Mobil/Image 2: 63
Mobil/Maclure: 56/57
Mobil/Stewart Bale: 59
Mobil/Thomas: 123

C. Newbould/Simons: 51, 52
C. Newbould/Trojan: 50/51
C. Newbould/J. Grant 52

Geoffrey Pass Photography: 116/117

Shell: 72, 73, 143

Texaco: 89, 92, 93, 95, 117, 120, 124, 130, 131, 144, 145, 146
Total: 97
Total/BR: 117
Total/J. Hicks: 98, 98/99, 99, 100
Total/R. Simmons: 97
Total/Peter Vintner: 145

Author's Collection: 13, 18, 43, 45, 53, 75, 101

AEC: 10, 12/13, 13, 16/17, 18, 19, 34, 35, 42, 43, 45, 50/51, 5, 56/57, 58, 59, 61, 62, 68, 70/71, 71, 77, 79, 80, 81, 83, 88, 89, 82, 93, 94, 97, 98, 99, 100, 111, 114, 115, 116, 118, 119, 120, 121, 122, 123, 124, 125, 131, 132, 134, 136, 142

Albion: 45, 50, 69, 71, 75, 79, 87, 138/139, 143

Armstrong-Saurer: 11

Associated Daimler: 59

Atkinson: 18, 32, 42, 43, 44, 50/51, 89, 90/91, 104, 124

Austin: 49, 60, 109, 111

Bedford: 29, 32, 33, 37, 38, 44, 59, 60, 61, 69, 71, 85, 86/87, 89, 104, 107, 111, 112/113, 135

Bristol: 6

Daf: 5, 21, 22, 22/23 100, 118

Dennis: 9, 11, 33, 70, 77, 78, 102, 106, 109, 121

Dodge: 42, 43, 44, 71, 97

ERF: 15, 32, 35, 62, 63, 82, 114, 119, 120, 131, 133, 134, 136, 140, 141, 145

Foden: 27, 32, 33, 35, 115, 143

Ford: 87, 93, 97

Fordson: 76

Guy: 83, 88, 92, 130

GV: 55

Halford: 49

International: 37, 105

Karrier: 7

Leyland: 14, 29, 30/31, 34, 39, 46, 47, 50/51, 53, 61, 62, 71, 73, 77, 78, 79, 81, 85, 88, 89, 93, 94, 95, 101, 103, 106, 114, 115, 116, 125, 132, 135, 140, 141, 142, 144, 146

Leyland-Daf: 23, 101

Maudslay: 38, 107

Mercedes: 47, 73, 137

Morris: 111, 125

Morris Commercial: 37, 39, 79, 109

Scammell: 28/29, 29, 59, 65, 67, 69, 70, 72, 74/75, 76, 80, 81, 82, 105, 107, 115, 123, 135

Scania: 94, 95, 136

Seddon Atkinson: 14, 15, 20, 35, 46, 47, 53, 63, 72, 73, 137

Thornycroft: 12, 40/41, 67, 68/69, 76, 107, 128

Volvo: 20, 22, 35, 51, 52, 53, 72, 95, 98, 99, 100

White: 26/27

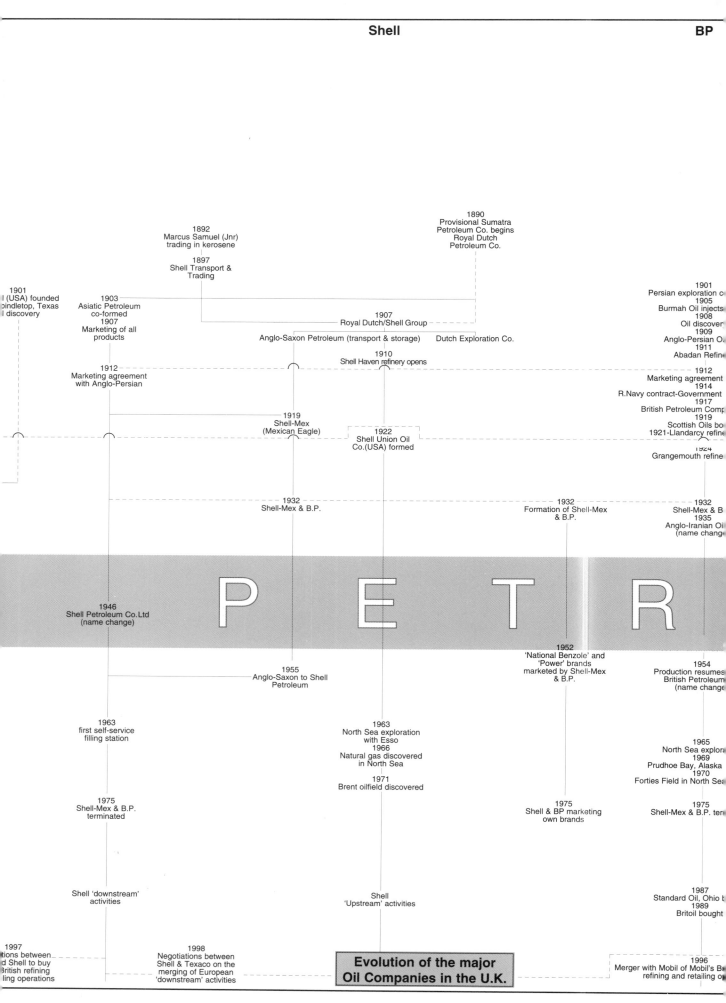

Shell   **BP**

1890
Provisional Sumatra
Petroleum Co. begins
Royal Dutch
Petroleum Co.

1892
Marcus Samuel (Jnr)
trading in kerosene

1897
Shell Transport &
Trading

1901
l (USA) founded
pindletop, Texas
l discovery

1901
Persian exploration c
1905
Burmah Oil injects
1908
Oil discover
1909
Anglo-Persian O
1911
Abadan Refin

1903
Asiatic Petroleum
co-formed
1907
Marketing of all
products

1907
Royal Dutch/Shell Group

Anglo-Saxon Petroleum (transport & storage)   Dutch Exploration Co.

1910
Shell Haven refinery opens

1912
Marketing agreement
with Anglo-Persian

1912
Marketing agreement
1914
R.Navy contract-Government
1917
British Petroleum Comp
1919
Scottish Oils bo
1921-Llandarcy refine

1919
Shell-Mex
(Mexican Eagle)

1922
Shell Union Oil
Co.(USA) formed

1924
Grangemouth refine

1932
Shell-Mex & B.P.

1932
Formation of Shell-Mex
& B.P.

1932
Shell-Mex & B
1935
Anglo-Iranian Oil
(name change

P E T R

1946
Shell Petroleum Co.Ltd
(name change)

1952
'National Benzole' and
'Power' brands
marketed by Shell-Mex
& B.P.

1954
Production resumes
British Petroleum
(name change

1955
Anglo-Saxon to Shell
Petroleum

1963
first self-service
filling station

1963
North Sea exploration
with Esso
1966
Natural gas discovered
in North Sea

1971
Brent oilfield discovered

1965
North Sea explora
1969
Prudhoe Bay, Alaska
1970
Forties Field in North Sea

1975
Shell-Mex & B.P.
terminated

1975
Shell & BP marketing
own brands

1975
Shell-Mex & B.P. ter

Shell 'downstream'
activities

Shell
'Upstream' activities

1987
Standard Oil, Ohio b
1989
Britoil bought

1997
tions between
d Shell to buy
British refining
ling operations

1998
Negotiations between
Shell & Texaco on the
merging of European
'downstream' activities

**Evolution of the major
Oil Companies in the U.K.**

1996
Merger with Mobil of Mobil's B
refining and retailing o

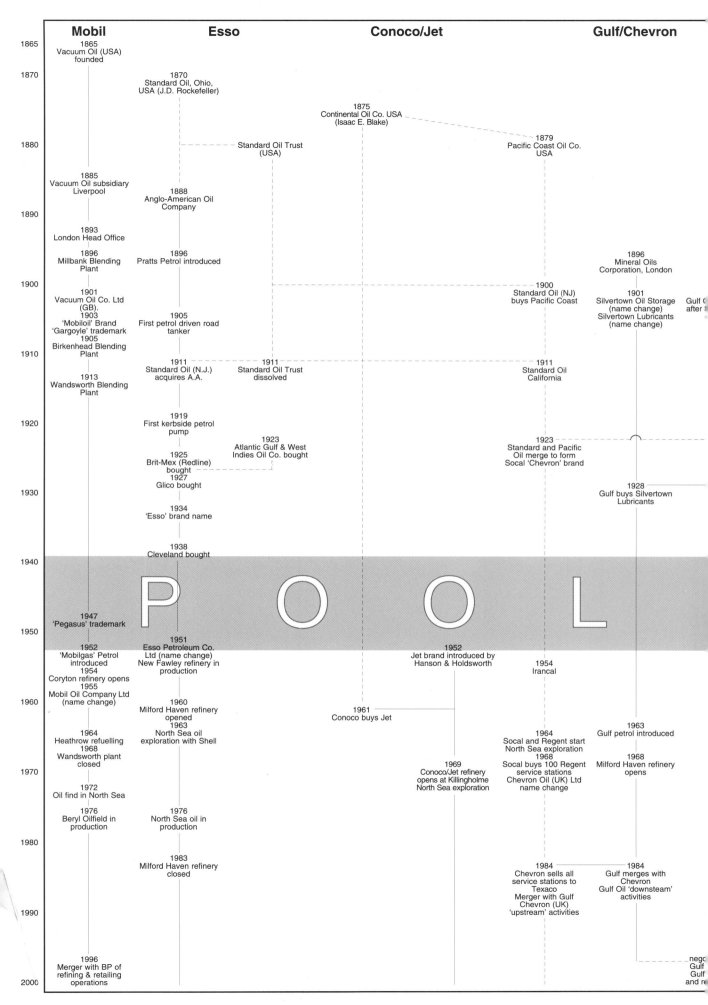

Year	Mobil	Esso	Conoco/Jet	Gulf/Chevron
1865	Vacuum Oil (USA) founded			
1870		Standard Oil, Ohio, USA (J.D. Rockefeller)		
1875			Continental Oil Co. USA (Isaac E. Blake)	
1879				Pacific Coast Oil Co. USA
1880		Standard Oil Trust (USA)		
1885	Vacuum Oil subsidiary Liverpool			
1888		Anglo-American Oil Company		
1893	London Head Office			
1896	Millbank Blending Plant	Pratts Petrol introduced		Mineral Oils Corporation, London
1900			Standard Oil (NJ) buys Pacific Coast	
1901	Vacuum Oil Co. Ltd (GB).			Silvertown Oil Storage (name change) Silvertown Lubricants (name change) / Gulf (after ...
1903	'Mobiloil' Brand 'Gargoyle' trademark			
1905	Birkenhead Blending Plant	First petrol driven road tanker		
1911		Standard Oil (N.J.) acquires A.A. / Standard Oil Trust dissolved		Standard Oil California
1913	Wandsworth Blending Plant			
1919		First kerbside petrol pump		
1923		Atlantic Gulf & West Indies Oil Co. bought		Standard and Pacific Oil merge to form Socal 'Chevron' brand
1925		Brit-Mex (Redline) bought		
1927		Glico bought		
1928				Gulf buys Silvertown Lubricants
1934		'Esso' brand name		
1938		Cleveland bought		

POOL

Year	Mobil	Esso	Conoco/Jet	Gulf/Chevron
1947	'Pegasus' trademark			
1951		Esso Petroleum Co. Ltd (name change) New Fawley refinery in production		
1952	'Mobilgas' Petrol introduced		Jet brand introduced by Hanson & Holdsworth	
1954	Coryton refinery opens			Irancal
1955	Mobil Oil Company Ltd (name change)			
1960		Milford Haven refinery opened		
1961			Conoco buys Jet	
1963		North Sea oil exploration with Shell		Gulf petrol introduced
1964	Heathrow refuelling			Socal and Regent start North Sea exploration
1968	Wandsworth plant closed			Socal buys 100 Regent service stations Chevron Oil (UK) Ltd name change / Milford Haven refinery opens
1969			Conoco/Jet refinery opens at Killingholme North Sea exploration	
1972	Oil find in North Sea			
1976	Beryl Oilfield in production	North Sea oil in production		
1983		Milford Haven refinery closed		
1984			Chevron sells all service stations to Texaco Merger with Gulf Chevron (UK) 'upstream' activities	Gulf merges with Chevron Gulf Oil 'downsteam' activities
1996	Merger with BP of refining & retailing operations			nego... / Gulf / Gulf / and re...